Forgive Me, Ma'am... Bears Don't Wear Blue

Larry Weill

with Kelly Weill

North Country Books, Inc.
Utica, New York

Forgive Me, Ma'am... Bears Don't Wear Blue
Copyright © 2009
by Larry Weill and Kelly Weill

ISBN-10 1-59531-030-4
ISBN-13 978-1-59531-030-9

Library of Congress Cataloging-in-Publication Data

Weill, Larry.
  Forgive me, ma'am-- bears don't wear blue / by Larry Weill & Kelly Weill.
     p. cm.
  ISBN 978-1-59531-030-9 (alk. paper)
  1. Weill, Larry. 2. Park rangers--New York (State)--Adirondack Park--
Biography. 3. New York (State). Dept. of Environmental Conservation--
Officials and employees--Biography. 4. Wilderness areas--New York (State)--
Adirondack Mountains--Anecdotes. 5. Wilderness area users--New York
(State)--Adirondack Mountains--Anecdotes. I. Weill, Kelly. II. Title.
  SB481.6.W45A3 2009
  363.6'8092--dc22
  [B]
                                            2009018843

North Country Books, Inc.
220 Lafayette Street
Utica, New York 13502
www.northcountrybooks.com

This book is dedicated to the lives of the Adirondack pioneers; to the guides, hunters, and trappers who blazed the trails that we now follow. Though gone in body, their spirits live on in every rise of Adirondack mountain and roar of Adirondack stream. May we all be blessed to follow in their footsteps and find the way.

Table of Contents

ADIRONDACK
STATE PARK

LAKE PLACID

RT. 30

NORTHVILLE
LAKE PLACID
TRAIL

OLD FORGE

SPECULATOR

NORTHVILLE

RT. 30

WEST
CANADA
CREEK
WILDERNESS
AREA

NEW YORK STATE

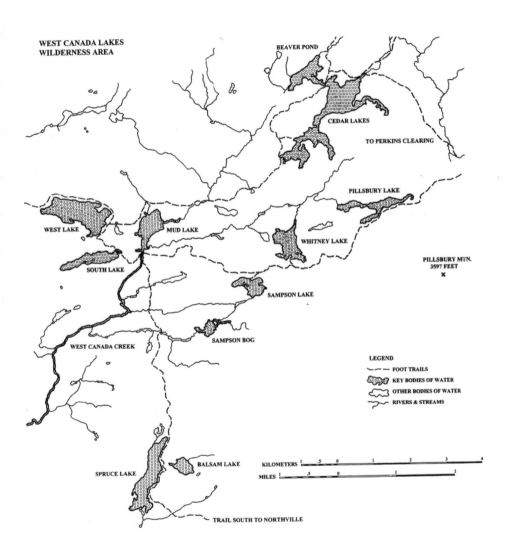

WEST CANADA LAKES
WILDERNESS AREA

BEAVER POND

CEDAR LAKES

TO PERKINS CLEARING

PILLSBURY LAKE

WEST LAKE

MUD LAKE

WHITNEY LAKE

PILLSBURY MTN.
3597 FEET
x

SOUTH LAKE

SAMPSON LAKE

WEST CANADA CREEK

SAMPSON BOG

LEGEND
--- FOOT TRAILS
KEY BODIES OF WATER
OTHER BODIES OF WATER
RIVERS & STREAMS

SPRUCE LAKE

BALSAM LAKE

KILOMETERS 1   .5   0   1   2   3   4
MILES 1   .5   0   1   2

TRAIL SOUTH TO NORTHVILLE

Acknowledgments

This book would not have been possible without the assistance of the many people who have aided me and provided me with healthy doses of inspiration over the years. These include Barbara Remias and other members of the Remias family, who assisted me with details of the caretakers' stations on Cedar and West Lakes. Barbara also provided biographical information on John, her beloved husband and my very good friend, who left us all too soon.

Several members of the wilderness park ranger program from the 1970s were instrumental in contributing their time and expertise to this book, including John Wood, Rick Miller, Tom Savage, C. Peter Fish, and Ben Woodard. Additionally, Tom Eakin, my boss from this period, provided me with the opportunity to work in this area and later served as an invaluable source of information about the territory and trails as they changed over the years.

I owe a debt of gratitude to Dr. John Klibanoff, my orthopedic surgeon in Rochester, New York, who took me apart and reassembled me with an artificial right hip. Without his incredibly skilled work, I would have been unable to return to the woods in 2007 with my daughter, which was the crowning event of my life in the woods. My unhampered mobility and (now) pain-free existence are due to his labors, for which I am incredibly grateful.

A special thanks goes out to a number of other professionals, including Rob Igoe, Jr., Zach Steffen, and all the wonderful people at North Country Books in Utica, New York. Without their guidance and encouragement over these past several years, none of this would have been possible.

The staffs of the libraries at the Department of Environmental Conservation in Albany and the Adirondack Museum library in Blue Mountain Lake have been wonderful in verifying facts as needed. Their ongoing assistance in this capacity insured the integrity of this book's content while saving me countless hours of research.

Finally, to my wife Patty; my daughters Kelly and Erin; my mother Bernice; and my sister Wendy, I extend the biggest thank you of all. Your continuous encouragement and support while traveling down this wonderful trail has been invaluable, and I am forever in your debt.

Introduction

I would like to start this book by saying "welcome back!" I am doing so because of the assumption I am making that most readers will have already finished at least one of the first two books in this series. Those books, titled *Excuse Me, Sir...Your Socks are on Fire* (2005), and *Pardon Me, Sir...There's a Moose in Your Tent* (2007), lay much of the groundwork for the stories contained inside this volume. That isn't to say that these stories run in any particular sequence, because they don't. You can start with this book, if you so desire, and read the others later. But some of the background descriptions of people and places have not been included here in order to avoid repetitive narrative.

When I address the audience of readers who are familiar with the West Canada Lakes Wilderness Area, either through actual visits or through the pages of these books, I feel a common bond. The woods, lakes, streams, and hills of this remote territory are not only unique in their natural beauty, but also very special to me for their familiarity as my "home." The people I met and camped with in this region will understand some of this emotion; they know what it's like to listen to the loons on Cedar Lakes, or to watch the deer graze the vegetation around Sampson Bog.

When I'm out there, I treasure the sights and sounds of the woods (which are still there for the taking), and I sense a very real connection with my past, especially when I am in the vicinity of landmarks such as the site of the old lean-to by the now-defunct Cedar Lakes Dam, or Adirondack French Louis' fireplace in the overgrown tangle of yard at West Lake. The mere sight of these remnants from earlier times triggers a torrent of sentimental emotions that is almost overwhelming. Hopefully, I have done a sufficient job of describing the people and events that made these places so special to me, thus enabling you to share in these vivid memories as I relive them myself.

I didn't start writing about my ranger adventures until long after I had left the woods. Approximately fourteen years had elapsed between the time I walked out of the West Canada Lakes on my last day of work and the time I wrote my first story. During those years, I served on active duty in the Navy, got married, and worked two (and sometimes three) jobs simultaneously. This left little or no room for writing, which I didn't begin in earnest until 1994. Then, after writing the material that would compose the first (and part of the second) book, I paused for another eight years before resuming this most enjoyable task.

Even after completing the second manuscript, (*Pardon Me, Sir...There's a Moose in Your Tent*), I felt as though I had a lot more to tell. There were stories from the woods that just couldn't be included without creating a monstrous-sized volume that wouldn't fit in a backpack. So, with renewed enthusiasm, I set out to create a third and final book on my years as a wilderness park ranger.

I must admit that this seemed like a daunting task at first, as I wondered whether I had used up my best stories in the first two books. However, as I laid out the structure for this edition and started to "fill in the branches" with tales from the woods, my worries quickly disappeared. I soon discovered that I would indeed experience storytelling problems, but from having too much to tell rather than not having enough.

As with both of the earlier volumes, these stories are passed along in a non-linear fashion. With the exception of the first and last chapters, I have intentionally scrambled the sequence of these episodes so that stories from years one, two, and three are interspersed with one another. I have also included a few amusing anecdotes that happened to me while I was outside the woods, usually somewhere between Glens Falls and Lake Placid. All of these do relate to the woods in some direct or indirect manner, with most of them taking place during my short Wednesday through Thursday "weekends."

I have also taken the liberty of using a small part of this book to describe my life on Mount Van Hoevenberg and my role in the Winter Olympics of 1980. This brief interlude in my life was a direct result of my years on the trails, as it served to fill the gap between the ranger seasons of 1979 and 1980. Because of the suggestion and influence of my good friend, John Giedraitis, I was offered a job that would allow me to see the Olympics up close and personal. This was the opportunity of a lifetime; the chance to see all the worlds' greatest winter athletes on the stage at the same time was irresistible.

Wholly contained inside the Adirondack Park, the Lake Placid Olympic facilities served as the backdrop for one of the most vivid seasons in my life. From watching the U.S. Olympic Hockey Team do the impossible, to "shovel sliding" at forty-plus miles per hour down the bobsled and luge runs, it was a magical time. The four chapters that describe these brief and fast-paced months are woven into the tapestry of my Adirondack memories, and they are inseparable from the experiences of my summer seasons on the trails.

Another very sentimental chapter of this book is one of the last ones written, as it involves my final trip through the West Canada Lakes territory and the first with my daughter Kelly. I've made no secret that these books were written primarily to document the events of my life as a younger man living a highly unusual existence amongst the woods and waters of the North Country. Because of a number of health issues, I always worried about being able to pass these stories along to my children—and I never really believed that I would have the opportunity to serve as a guide for my older daughter, especially once my hip went bad.

My luck changed when, due to the miracles of modern medicine,

I received an amazingly successful hip transplant in 2005. After a relatively brief recovery period, I was able to complete a voyage that would have been impossible just a few years earlier. With a full pack containing all of the weight of my own supplies, plus some for my daughter, I walked (complete with my titanium hip parts) over the same path I had wandered as a wilderness park ranger. To say that this was a pleasant experience would be an understatement. Anyone who has suffered through the pains of a badly arthritic hip joint knows just how painful and debilitating that can be. Even a simple stroll down the street, carrying nothing but your own weight, can be a long and tedious process. The thought of completing a thirty mile journey over rough and wet terrain would have been ludicrous.

When I posed the possibility of this trip to Kelly, she immediately jumped at the opportunity. Having read both of the first two books of this series, and also having had a hand in proofreading the second volume, she was positively thrilled at the thought of seeing this land for herself.

Yet I knew that there might be problems. For example, the week that we had reserved for the trip was the one that immediately followed our summer vacation aboard a luxury cruise ship, touring throughout the warm and bug-free waters of the Caribbean Sea, with lots of sun, sand, cold drinks, and opulent surroundings in every port. And the next stop? The wet, hot, dirty, sweaty, buggy trails of the West Canada Lakes Wilderness Area. The comparison was, I knew, too much for the uninitiated mind to fathom, so I said nothing and prepared Kelly for a beautiful stroll in the woods. (Yes, I did mention the biting insects.)

Regardless of the tough conditions, we were able to complete the trip as planned, which introduced her to the very best that our region had to offer. We spent four days and three nights doing "Standard Trip #1," which included the trail from Perkins Clearing to Cedar Lakes, through the West Canadas, then off to Sampson and Pillsbury Lakes, then back out to Perkins Clearing.

The trip was a resounding success, and Kelly performed like a champ. I'm not proud to have to admit that a thirteen year-old was often waiting for me to catch up on the trails. However, as I was carrying the weight AND the artificial hip, I really didn't feel too badly about that fact, and we both made it through in fine shape.

To me, it is quite significant that this book ends with the chapter about my return trip through the woods with Kelly. The reason for this is simple: with this endeavor, I feel as though my time in the woods (and with these books) has come full circle. My love of the woods, and specifically *these* woods, is something that I always wanted to pass down to the next generation. Rather than having to do so through the pages of a book, I had the chance to do so live, in person, father-to-daughter. I hope to have the same chance someday with my younger daughter, Erin, as well, assuming that I have the good fortune of maintaining a sound, healthy body.

I'd like to extend a heartfelt thanks to everyone who has chosen to share some time with me by reading the stories contained in these volumes. The people and events recorded in them are very near and dear to me, as are the Adirondack woodlands we have in common. Equally important to me is the task of introducing our children to these woods, so that the love of this national treasure can be passed on from generation to generation. It is my sincerest hope that these episodes might spark that interest in the minds of our little ones, so that they might start dreaming of their own Adirondack adventures. If I am able to accomplish both these missions through the pages of these books, then my pilgrimage is complete, and I am truly a lucky man.

—1—

Introducing Kelly

This section was written by Kelly Weill shortly after our excursion through the West Canada Lakes region in 2007.

To this day I am extremely flattered that someone would write a book on my behalf. That was the initial concept my father had in mind when he wrote his first book: to provide me with a written record of his days as a wilderness park ranger. Dad knew that his job was unique and that there were great stories to tell because of it. He also knew that he wanted these stories to be preserved. Since the time he recorded these first episodes (when I was an infant), I have grown to the age at which I can not only read and love these stories, but also hike in the same woods and see the territory for myself.

The woods and the people my father grew to know there have always meant a lot to him. Even though his ranger days are long past, he still talks of them often. But the woods he knew are much different today. Many of his friends who worked in this region are now gone. One such person was John Remias, Dad's good friend and the interior caretaker at Cedar Lakes and later, at West Lake. I wish I could have met John, because my father has told me so much about him. En route to our trip through the West Canada Lakes, we visited his widow, Barbara Remias, who still lives in the region and helped with the preparation of this book. Barbara talked about John during our brief visit, and she obviously still misses him, even though he has been gone for over fifteen years. John's hat and coat still hang on a nail at the back door of Barbara's house, as though he had left them there just yesterday.

My interest in the territory began when I read the first book, *Excuse Me, Sir...Your Socks are on Fire*. I reread it several times, intrigued by the stories of the woods and the odd situations in which my father found himself on a regular basis. I was quite young (and still am today), but I thought that it would be a great place to visit when I was old enough to make the trip. Being an aspiring writer myself, I was impressed by the fact that my father's stories were already in print.

By the time the second book was released, I was old enough to help Dad by proofreading and editing the manuscript. The new stories caused my interest in the region to grow even further. It also sparked my interest in writing similar material, as my father and I shared our love of writing and the Adirondack Park.

For many years, Dad and I had agreed that it would be nice to go together into the West Canada Lakes to see his old ranger territory. Shortly after the release of *Pardon Me, Sir...There's a Moose in Your Tent*, we began to plan such a trip. Dad referred to it as a "last call" visit because he had been slowed considerably by a deteriorating hip joint that had required a complete replacement about two years earlier. Before the surgery, he was unsure if he would be able to make the trek at all, as the consequences of getting stuck in the woods with a stiff joint could be dangerous. Luckily, the surgery was a complete success, and he now proclaims himself to be a "walking advertisement for hip replacements."

As the expedition began to take shape and we started to collect supplies, I began to feel some doubt about my ability to complete such an arduous voyage. The pack I was given to carry was huge and seemed to grow every day, as more and more supplies were added to it. Although I have been involved in athletics and organized sports for most of my life, I had never had to carry any kind of a load on my back for any period of time (with the possible exception of my backpack with a full complement of text books). Dad would be carrying the majority of the weight in his huge Kelty pack, but everything else (my clothes, sleeping bag, flashlight, and food) would be in my pack. Whenever I picked it up experimentally, it seemed to weigh more than I did.

We decided to prepare for the trip by taking a short "conditioning hike" in a nearby park. Dad and I brought our packs and filled them so that their weights would be similar to what we would carry in the woods. I accomplished this by filling my bag with plastic dumbbells. This turned out to be a bad idea, as they shifted during the hike, pushing uncomfortably against my spine. However, for the most part, we both felt great for the two miles of the trail and decided that we were capable of the excursion into the West Canadas.

Both of us were extremely pleased that we were able to make this trip. Because I'd read the first two books without seeing the territory, I had mental images of the landscape, most of which were incorrect. If anything, the woods and lakes were more beautiful than I had imagined. Through the first two volumes, I was able to associate locations with events that happened there decades earlier. I recognized the location where Dad had first met John Remias, the spot where he had watched the exhausted Boy Scout fall into the lake, and the place where two bears crossed his path simultaneously. At one point on the trail, Dad remarked that it was a bit unnerving that I already knew the stories that he told about certain locations. For me, it just added to the fun of seeing the woods firsthand.

This, my father's final installment, adds new dimensions to his series. It includes some stories from the West Canada Lakes that were both interesting and amusing, but simply would not fit into the first two books. Additionally, it contains four chapters describing my father's days on Mount Van Hoevenburg as a member of the bobsled and luge track crew for the 1980 Olympics. He took this job when his seasonal job in the West Canada Lakes was over for the winter. All of the stories are as funny as they are fascinating (although I still can't imagine the thought of two hundred bottles of beer sliding down a bobsled run!) and were never discussed in either of the first two books.

Finally, on a more personal level, this book has greatly increased my own interest in the Adirondack Park and the pursuit of Adirondack writing. Although I have always possessed an interest in both these areas, my father's offer to guide me through this part of his past has changed the way I see these woods. I discovered the Adirondacks he loves and the people who remain his friends today. I am grateful for the introduction and hope that you enjoy these stories as much as my father has enjoyed telling them.

—2—

Wrong Turn at Sled Harbor

I must admit that I was looking forward to my second week in the woods with great anticipation. After all, my first week included some experiences that I'd rather not relive, including almost blacking out on the trail and going for a full-body bath in the swamp near Sucker Brook. I had left a lot of room for improvement, and I was ready to have a go at it.

Another reason I wanted to get back into the woods was to meet one of the local celebrities, a semi-hermit by the name of Leighton Slack. My predecessor from the previous year, Ben Woodard, had told me all about Leighton, who lived alone in a small camp past Perkins Clearing, down a logging road that turned off of Route 30 about eight miles north of Speculator.

All I knew about Leighton was that he was in his seventies and had just gone back to live in the woods because he didn't care for life in the city, or even in a small town like Speculator. Ben had told me that Leighton would gladly watch my car for me while I was in the woods and that he'd be good conversation when I returned.

What I didn't realize was that Leighton was very unlike the

5

stereotypical "hermit" of old-time stories, those individuals who defended their privacy fiercely when necessary. From the very first day I met Leighton, he appeared to be the exact opposite. He was a charming soul with lively blue eyes that danced when he told me his stories of the woods and the people who visited them. His wonderful personality just attracted people to him, and, in essence, made his "hermitness" a moot point, because he was very seldom alone in his cabin in the woods.

The very first time I pulled up to his cabin, I knew we were going to be friends. Leighton invited me inside and generously shared coffee and cake with me while plying me with stories of the area. He was an avid talker, and I listened to his tales while looking around his kitchen and out at his yard. He was an ardent car enthusiast and had several older-model vehicles sitting around in front of his cabin in various stages of repair. Car calendars hung in his kitchen, and he expounded on the advantages of the different engine types he had repaired over the decades, going back to the early days of automotive assembly.

Leighton was fascinating, and I quickly fell under his spell, listening in rapt attention. In fact, if it weren't for my vague awareness of the time, I could have stayed there all day. However, I knew that I had a ten mile stretch of trail ahead of me that I'd never hiked before. Better to get going now, in case I ran into any difficulties along the way.

I bid farewell to my new friend after parking my beat up Oldsmobile under a tree in his yard. Then I hoisted my pack onto my back and started the trek into Cedar Lakes via the Perkins Clearing-Sled Harbor trail. For those hikers who are not interested in hiking the Northville-Lake Placid trail, this is probably the most popular route in the area for reaching Cedar Lakes. It was fairly direct, only about nine miles long, and contained very little in the way of rough climbing.[1]

I made my way past the locked gate and headed on down the

[1] Since the time this story took place, the position of the Perkins Clearing (Sled Harbor) gate has been moved forward. It is now possible to park a car within about five miles of Cedar Lakes.

wide logging road. It was as wide as any city street, with a hard dirt-gravel base that could easily withstand the daily grind of the heavy logging trucks which traveled it in route to their cutting sites. It wasn't uncommon to be hiking along this trail and have to skip up onto an embankment to allow one of these behemoths to rumble past. They were huge and carried impressive loads of logs.

The map was easy to read: just follow this road for a mile until it crosses over the Miami River. At that point, I would see the Miami River lean-to on the left side of the road. (I never did understand the logic of building a lean-to right along this road. Never in three years did I see anyone camping inside this structure.) Then, the next marker would be a turnoff to the right, about another mile down the logging road, where it would turn into a trail for Cedar Lakes. Piece of cake, right?

Within the next hour, all that I saw was a fork in the road, where a side road turned to the right and the major logging road continued. Since the turnoff was obviously another logging road and not a hiking path, I decided to continue straight. I walked on, making pretty good time and enjoying the splendid stands of hardwood trees as they towered high above my head. I found that by staying in the middle of the road, I was able to avoid some of the larger flocks of blackflies and mosquitoes that lay in ambush by the roadside. That was some consolation, anyway, for the fact that I could not seem to locate the trail.

The logging road bent to the left, then to the right, then up hills, then down hills. On and on and on I walked, all the while knowing that something was wrong. Where the heck was I? Could they possibly have enlarged the trails into roads? No, I knew that wasn't the case. I also knew that I must be miles beyond my intended turnoff, and yet on I walked.

I think it was the lowering of the sun in the sky that made me decide that enough was enough. I had obviously walked off into a different part of New York State, and I wasn't going another step further. At least in that direction. As a matter of fact, I quickly reasoned that I had reached a logical place to spend the night. So with my tail between my legs, I disappeared into the woods off the road and quickly pitched my tent, ready to start back as early as possible the next morning. I looked over my maps again, trying to figure out just where I had gone wrong. The best I could tell was that I had turned west somewhere and may have hiked all the way through to a location close to the Jessup River. But I couldn't be sure.

The sun rose early the following day, and I was up with the first rays. It was only my second week on the job, and here I was, the ranger, lost and miles off track. I clearly didn't feel too good about it. After wolfing down some breakfast bars and a quick cup of cocoa, I hit the road, this time in a reciprocal direction from the previous afternoon. I figured that if I really hoofed it, I could make it back to the real trailhead by sometime before noon and reach the Cedar Lakes dam by 2:00-3:00 P.M. It was a plan that depended on strong legs and few breaks, but I thought I could do it.

I was getting into my stride, just starting to feel good about my chances of getting back on schedule, when I first felt, then heard, the ultra-bass vibration of a big engine, distinctive in its sound. As the massive logging truck chugged down the road, still over a half mile away, I could feel the power in the engine as it pulled its payload of timber from the woods.

The truck seemed to take a long time to approach; when it finally came upon my spot, it slowed down and came to a stop. I walked around to the other side of the cab to see what the driver needed.

A friendly face under a yellow ball cap peered down from the driver's side window. "Hey, you need a ride?" the logger asked, speaking through a rugged and sunburned smile.

"I'd be happy to take you up on that offer," I replied, just as rapidly as I could speak. "I'm heading back towards Sled Harbor."

"I'm going that way myself. Hop in and throw your pack in the back. Anything for an employee of the state."

Wow! My day had suddenly improved immeasurably, and I wasn't able to say another word. I climbed the several steps required to reach the cab compartment, then heaved my pack in behind the front seat.

The logger, who must have worked back there for years, was used to seeing rangers as they trekked up to Sled Harbor and headed off into the woods. But this gentleman was clearly interested in my route; what was I doing all the way out in the middle of nowhere like that?

"No, it's not someplace that's on my official route," I explained. (At least that part was true.) "But we've had some issues with campers using non-designated areas for pitching tents and damaging equipment back there, so I just wanted to check it out. Now I'm on my way back to Sled Harbor."

The trucker, whose name I never did get, nodded in thoughtful silence. Either he believed me fully, or he just didn't care. But as we rolled along over the dusty roads I had hiked just a day earlier, I thanked my lucky stars that I was getting this free lift. After a trip that lasted for at least a half hour, my new friend pulled his truck to a stop at a big clearing in the road. I recognized it as the very first turnoff that I had passed the previous morning. The trucker said his final farewell and rumbled off into the distance, headed towards one of the many logging mills down south.

As I shouldered my pack, I took some careful mental notes about my surroundings. A more sharp-eyed view into the woods allowed me to see a single painted arrow, which was nailed to an obscured tree trunk. The rest of the trail sign, which included directions and distances to Cedar Lakes, Pillsbury Lake, and the West Canadas, lay on the ground, obviously pulled off by some unscrupulous character. I made a mental note to have someone come back this way and rehang it in a more conspicuous location.

OK, this was more like it! It was barely past 7:00 A.M., and I was already back to Sled Harbor and on my way. I knew things could only get better from here and that I had very few remaining opportunities to lose myself in these woods. After all, we only had about three different weekly routes, and I had already covered two of them. I only had one more chance to get lost, and that would be the following week when I had to come up from the south, through Piseco and Spruce Lake. But I wasn't going to worry about that quite yet.

The next couple of hours flew by as I sped my way up Blue Ridge, past the turnoffs for Pillsbury Mountain Fire Tower and Pillsbury Lake. It was still sometime before 10:30 A.M. when I looked ahead of me and saw someone approaching on the trail. That person wore a uniform just like mine and carried most of the same equipment.

John Wood! My partner in the territory was hiking the trail from Cedar Lakes over to Sampson and was clearly interested in my tardy appearance.

"Hi Larry," he said, looking at me from under his green, state-issued cap. "I thought I'd see you here yesterday."

It was more of a question than a statement, and I briefly considered repeating my little white lie of earlier. However, I quickly decided to confess the error of my previous day, hoping that he wouldn't pass it along to our boss.

John was obviously amused at the distance I had hiked beyond the appointed turnoff. He had always been a hiker and naturalist, with a huge amount of experience walking the trails of the Adirondacks. To him, my actions must have seemed quite absurd. However, he maintained his self-control and never appeared to laugh at me.

We traded stories and experiences from our first week in the woods, and I warned him about the exertion required on the Sucker Brook trail that I had hiked during the first week. He filled me in on the route through Cedar Lakes and the various places where I could expect to find campers. Then we parted ways, as he moved towards Sampson and I resumed my trek towards the dam on Cedars.

It wasn't long before I emerged at the large wooden dam that crossed over the northeast end of the lake. I removed my pack and looked around, glad that I had recovered from my navigational error with a minimum of damage and exertion. At least now I was on familiar ground, since I would be retracing my steps of the previous week. It felt good, and my confidence level soared.

As I marched along the northern shore of the lake, I approached the Beaver Pond lean-to, or what some folks used to call Cedar Lakes lean-to #2. I could see at a distance that it was occupied by a small hiking group, so I decided to stop by for a chat.

The hiking group was composed of three young men, all of whom were in their late twenties. These were "through hikers" who were doing the entire length (134 miles) of the Northville-Lake Placid Trail. They were clearly impressed with their surroundings and stuck with the familiar problem that through-hikers often face. Here was a spot that was so beautiful that they desired to stop for a few days and just take in the scenery. Yet their schedule locked them into the daily grind of covering fifteen miles, then moving on without a day's rest. I could understand their dilemma, because the Beaver Pond lean-to was my idea of the perfect camping location.

One of the men, a tall fellow with curly brown hair and a beard to match, introduced himself as Mike. He wanted to know if there was a quick way to come back in to this spot without following the Placid Trail all the way up from Piseco (a distance of about twenty-three to twenty-four miles).

"Yes, there are numerous other routes you can follow," I advised him. "Several of them will get you here in a single day; there's no need to hike all the way up from Piseco. Probably the easiest of all is the road into Perkins Clearing, which I just used today."

Mike wanted to hear more about this possibility. "Is this a well-marked trail, or just a path that the locals know about? I'd rather stick to the major trails that we can follow easily on our maps."

I was born to never tell a lie, and I would be the last person to hide any information that might put someone off course in the woods. Yet I couldn't help but think that anyone but me would have seen the sign pointing the way to Cedar Lakes yesterday. After a brief internal debate, I quickly decided to hide my own ineptitude and send him via the Sled Harbor trail.

"Oh, not a problem," I said breezily, waving my hand in the air. "All you have to do is to head straight back along the logging road about two miles, then follow the turn-off at Sled Harbor. There's a big yellow arrow nailed to a tree that points the way. You can hardly miss it!"

—3—

The Honeymooners

It was the week of the big rains—perhaps not the wettest week I ever encountered on the trails, as I'd seen some pretty impressive floods, but it ranked in the top five, which said a lot. What marked it as being a little unusual was that it came in the middle of June, which was the start of what was ordinarily the dry period. Then again, nothing ever surprised me about the weather in the Adirondack Mountains. It could (and usually would) change three or four times in any twenty-four-hour period, leaving hikers playing a continuous guessing game on what to pack and what to wear.

On this particular week, I had hiked in from Perkins Clearing in the middle of a torrential downpour. Normally, I'd wait an hour or two longer before starting my journey into the woods on Friday morning, just to see if the weather would clear. But today the skies showed no promise whatsoever of breaking up; the gray blanket overhead was thick and low. The oppressive rain seemed to add fifteen pounds to the weight of my pack.

Actually, my feelings about the whole phenomenon of getting wet while hiking changed over time. At first, I went out of my way to avoid hiking in the really wet stuff, but after my first few months in the woods, it just didn't seem to matter anymore. Wet, dry, hot, cool, it was all the same. However, I always found that the first day out each week was a little different. I would often take rather extraordinary measures to stay dry as long as possible, including wearing a poncho when it wasn't necessary and tip-toeing daintily around the puddles that formed in the middle of the trail.

But not today. There was no room between the raindrops to hide, and the puddles had merged into a solid, deep pond that seemed to flow across the entire width of the trail. Even the places that were never wet had rivers of water swish-swashing their way along the path. The water soon soaked into my boots until it was up to my ankles. Each step I took resulted in a deep sucking noise, as my foot sank down into the black ooze before being yanked back up. It was wet.

I passed a couple of parties coming out of the woods, in route back to Perkins Clearing. Understandably, none of them felt like standing around chatting for very long. (Then again, they may not have recognized my uniform underneath the hooded poncho and pack cover.) But just as well; I had miles to go and didn't feel much like talking. I knew that the "dry spots" would be wet, the wet spots would be flooded, and the normally flooded stretches of trail might require some creative backstroking!

I bypassed the old lean-to down at the Cedar Lakes dam in favor of the one at Beaver Pond. I'd always found that the Beaver Pond lean-to was nicer in rainy weather. It was up on slightly higher ground and was just a little bit brighter. It was also closer to the loons, which tended to hang out near the little bridge over the Beaver Pond inlet. I never could resist listening to their songs at night and watching them fish during the day.

As I strolled down the final path to the lean-to, I noticed that I had company. The lean-to was empty, but a solitary orange tent was set up about twenty feet away, quietly repelling the non-stop droplets of rain. It was a nice tent made by a quality manufacturer and could easily hold two people on an extended trip. But the tent was zipped shut, and no one appeared to be coming out to say hello, so I ignored it and went about the process of unpacking.

For the next hour, I spent my time setting up my stuff for the night and moving some semi-dry firewood into the lean-to. Since it was a bit chilly, I got my stove going and made myself a cup of tea, all the while casting an occasional glance over at the tent, which still sat silently in the clearing. After all, this was a bit unusual. Perhaps they were off on a day hike? I really doubted that, because very few people willingly hiked in such weather. Also, even fewer people were willing to leave their things behind like that, for fear of "two legged predators" (translate to "people") walking off with their stuff. Maybe they were taking a nap? And why hadn't they claimed the lean-to, since nobody else was around? Most of the time, even people who carry a tent with them would rather sleep in a lean-to, given the choice.

Oh well, it was of no matter to me, although I was curious. I went about my normal routine, then started to get ready for my evening meal. I had just lit my stove again and was adjusting the flame when I heard the unmistakable sound of a zipper. Aha—there was life within the tent!

Shortly thereafter, a young bearded fellow, mid-twentyish, stooped through the opening between the flaps and stepped into the clearing by the fireplace. He appeared to be blinking the sleep out of his eyes while getting used to the daylight.

"Hi," I said with a smile, "I was wondering whether there was anyone in there, or whether the tent was available for rent!"

"We couldn't help it," the young man replied. "We were both up quite late last night and got a case of the 'sleepies' this afternoon. I guess we dozed off for longer than expected. It looks like it's almost time for chow."

"Yeah, it is," I said, "but I don't think it will be very easy to get a fire going in this downpour. I'm cooking in the lean-to, and you're welcome to join me. For that matter, you can move your gear inside and sleep in there. It'd probably be a lot more comfortable. Are there just two of you?"

"Yes," he answered. "My name is John, and my bride inside the tent is Jennie. She should be climbing out of the tent any month now."

"Your bride?" I asked in amazement. "When were you married?"

"Friday of last week," John replied. "We spent a few days with our family and then headed up here for our honeymoon. It's been really nice, although we could do with a bit less rain and a bit more sunshine."

John sat down on the front of the lean-to with me and within a few minutes was joined by his new wife. Actually, Jennie didn't "climb" out of the tent. Instead, it looked as though she had been shot out by an unseen cannon, landing underneath the overhanging roof of the lean-to with very few intermediate steps. It was obvious that she didn't want to get wet.

"Hey, hon," John murmured as the young woman landed in his lap, "I was just talking to the ranger here about our honeymoon. I hope we didn't awaken you?"

"Oh no," replied Jennie, who looked a bit out of place in these surroundings. "I had to get up in order to see the rest of this rainstorm. I wouldn't have wanted to miss that for the world!" The statement was issued with more than a small dose of sarcasm.

Sitting back preparing my meal, I quietly chuckled at the difference between the two newlyweds. I didn't know them from Adam, yet I thought they looked distinctly mismatched. John looked very much the woodsman, with a thick wool shirt and an equally thick growth of black beard covering his face. His very persona seemed to project a certain comfort with the surroundings, as though he had grown up in the woods. Jennie, on the other hand, appeared to be a refined woman who would rather be in a more urban setting. Her streaked blond hair and high cheek bones would have been better suited in a designer dress than the blue jeans and white knit sweater in which she was clad. She was also one of the only women I had ever met in the woods who was wearing lipstick, which lent even more glamour to her appearance. She clearly didn't fit in with the West Canada Lakes "resort" theme.

John quickly introduced me to his new wife, who sat down by his side.

"Well, from the sound of it, you're not enthralled with our climate," I said to Jennie. "Is this the first time you've been out in the woods back here?"

"I've been to the Adirondacks plenty of times," she replied. "But this is the first time I've gone hiking like this, so far back in the woods. I had sort of hoped that we'd do something in the Caribbean, but we just couldn't afford it this year, so John talked me into this as an alternate honeymoon. We're hoping to be able to go to the Bahamas within the next year or two, and I'll probably call that our real honeymoon."

I had to laugh at that one. Let me see: the Bahamas versus Cedar Lakes. It didn't sound like much of a contest for a couple of honeymooners, although I loved the West Canadas myself. I decided to keep out of that debate, instead focusing on cooking the rest of my meal.

As I used my knife to whittle a bit of cheddar cheese onto the top of my chili dish, I overheard bits and snatches of John and Jennie's conversation as they moved about the site. They too were setting up for dinner, transporting their stove and dishes into the lean-to. John pulled a large cook pot out of a stuff sack. He held it up with just his thumb and index finger, as though he didn't want to touch it, all the while looking at it in a rather disgusted manner.

"Honey, did you put this pot away last night?" John asked. "It was never washed! It's got the remains of beef burgundy and rice stuck to the bottom."

"No, I didn't clean it because I cooked last night, remember? It was your turn to clean. And I didn't put it away, either. I think you did that after it got dark."

"No, sweetheart, that wasn't what we decided on," John countered. "I cooked and cleaned on Wednesday night over at West Lake, then last night you were supposed to. Remember...I even got all the wash water ready for you even though it was your turn."

"It was not my turn," Jennie said patiently. "It was your turn, because I did everything the night before."

I couldn't remain silent a moment longer. "Give me the pan and I'll wash it," I said, feigning a degree of exasperation. "You can call it my wedding present to the both of you!"

"No, that's OK," John said with a smile. "We're just kidding. It really doesn't matter who does the dishes. We just like giving each other a hard time."

As John got ready to wash the pot, he pulled an old bandana and a bar of green striped deodorant soap from a sack. Then he dumped a bit of water from a tin can into the cook pot and started scrubbing.

"Is that your dish soap?" I asked incredulously, looking at the scented bar. "Looks like you'll have the best smelling dishes in town!"

"Yeeeeaaaahhhh," John replied, drawing the word out over a long stretch of time as though he wanted to make a point. "It wasn't supposed to be. I actually purchased a bottle of the super-duper, environmentally friendly, biodegradable dish soap. It's just that it never made it into the pack *like it was supposed to*!" Those last few words were undoubtedly directed at Jennie, who looked up with an exasperated expression.

"Well, if you had bothered to look in the last bag on the back seat, then you'd have your soap and I'd have my extra socks, and we'd both be happy."

"I asked you if there was anything left back there and you

never answered me."

"I never heard you."

"What do you mean 'you never heard me?' We were both in the same car."

Huh. This had the potential to get out of hand, but there was very little that I could do. Since I had no real desire to take a walk in the rain, I was sort of stuck. So instead I reverted to an old ploy; I switched the topic. I migrated over to a theme that usually got couples going: I asked about how they met. This hit a real soft spot with John and Jennie, and for the next ten to fifteen minutes the two of them told me they had been high school sweethearts before going their own ways, only to get back together at a later time. By the time we turned in, the peace had been completely restored, and the two of them headed into their tent holding hands, their eyes filled with marital bliss.

It rained the entire night through and hadn't stopped in the morning when I packed up my gear and broke camp. Although it was past 9:00 A.M. by the time I finally left, my two new friends had still not shown themselves. Ah well, it was their honeymoon, and honeymoons never lend themselves to early mornings. No wonder they had chosen to sleep in a tent rather than a public lean-to. I smiled as I hoisted my pack onto my back for the walk down to West Lake, silently saying goodbye to John and Jeannie. I wished that they'd have a good life together and that they would eventually make it to the Bahamas. Without arguing!

The hike down to West Lake that morning was memorable, with the wet stuff cascading down through the trees. On some days, when it had been dry for a period of time and we received a light shower, very little rain actually made it to the ground. Instead, the leaves in the upper canopies seemed to soak up a good amount, and I could make it to my destination while remaining fairly dry. On those occasions, I never even bothered donning rain gear, as I'd get wetter from the resulting sweat than from the rain. But not today.

As I finally squished my way through the tall grass in back of John Remias' interior caretaker's cabin, I felt the familiar sensation of water filling my boots to the ankle. Each step forced air out through the tops of my boots, making a hissing sound that could be heard at quite a distance. Additionally, I felt the water running in small streams down my back. Whether it was from sweat or precipitation at this point made very little difference. It didn't feel great, and I looked forward to stopping into John's cabin for a lengthy period of drying out.

As I stomped around to the front of the cabin, I noticed that the weather must have been a bit much even for John. I knew that he was inside because of the smoke coming from the top of the chimney, but the front door was closed tight to keep out the cool dampness that had saturated the air. I couldn't blame him, as I would have stayed inside the whole day myself had my schedule permitted.

I never bothered knocking, as I saw John rising from the wooden chair that he kept next to the front window. He opened the door and looked at me with a combination of amusement and pity.

"Well, if it isn't the local neighborhood trail stalker," he cackled. "You look like a drowned rat! Come in and dry off."

I needed no persuading. I quickly dumped my pack next to the door and hung my poncho above it, noticing the river of rainwater that cascaded down its length, forming its own puddle on the porch stones.

"What the heck are you doing on the trail on a day like today?" John asked. "It's not like you'll see anyone on the move. Those hikers never like to get their feet wet while getting their wilderness experience!"

"I know, but what am I supposed to do?" I said. "I can't sit in the same lean-to for the whole week. I'd go out of my mind! Besides, I can get dried off pretty quickly, assuming that I can get out of the rain for the afternoon and into another lean-to. I really don't mind."

John put up coffee and threw an extra log into the wood-burning stove to add more heat to the room. I took advantage of the warmth by removing my boots and socks, placing the boots at a sufficient distance from the stove to warm slowly and hanging my socks on a hook in back of the stove to dry. I noticed with amusement that they soon began emitting wisps of steam as the heat pulled the moisture out of the material.

"So what's going on down at Cedars?" John asked, as he stirred some sugar into the coffee. "Got many people down there today?"

"Nah, it's pretty quiet," I answered. "I saw a couple of people going out to their cars on Friday, and then I camped with a couple of newlyweds last night over by the Beaver Pond. Besides that, it's been desolate."

John looked at me with a thoughtful expression. "Newlyweds?" he asked. "Medium-sized guy with a beard and a pretty blond-haired girl with fancy clothes?"

"Yes!" I replied. "That's them. I camped next to their tent last night. Would you believe it—they've only been married a week! They had wanted to go to the Bahamas but couldn't afford it, so they're using this as their honeymoon instead."

John gazed out the window at the rain as he lit another cigarette, the smoke curling up around his short grey hair.

"Some week for a honeymoon!" he said, laughing as he spoke. "You know, those two only stopped by here for a couple of minutes, and they never said anything about being newlyweds. But there was something about them that made me think that anyway. They had that special look between the two of them, like they were communicating on a different level. They looked like a couple of love-struck puppies."

"I know what you mean," I said. "They stayed in their tent almost the entire time I was down there. But you know, the funny thing was, they sure did argue a lot for a couple on their honeymoon. You know, silly things, like who forgot to pack what, and who should do the dishes."

That set John off into a fit of laughter. "Oh my God, yes! She was giving him hell down here because her feet were wet, and he forgot to bring along her extra pair of dry socks. I thought she was going to strangle him!"

"Yeah, I heard about that, too, down at Cedars. Pretty bad week to forget the spare socks, huh?"

I spent the next couple of hours in John's cabin, drying off and enjoying the conversation. There was something about John that made him fun to be with. He was as knowledgeable as anyone I'd ever known about the ways of the woods, and he was willing to give you the shirt off his back. Yet, in some way, I felt something more, almost as though he had become my surrogate father for the three years that I lived between the lakes of the West Canadas. I thoroughly enjoyed being with him and was never in a hurry to leave.

It never did stop raining until the following Tuesday morning. By then, I had circled around past Sampson, Whitney, and Pillsbury Lakes and had made the up-and-back patrol to Cedar River Flow. By that time, John and Jennie had long since left the woods and headed back to their home in the city. As a matter of fact, I saw almost no one for the entire remainder of the week, which wasn't surprising due to the continuous downpour. I would imagine that anyone who had plans to come in for the weekend would have cancelled them. Even the "through hikers" who would be going from Northville all the way up to Lake Placid seemed to have resigned themselves to the elements and hunkered down in a lean-to for the duration. It was desolate.

Tuesday morning... my last day in the woods before hiking out for my "weekend." I arose quite early and immediately noticed that the rain had ceased and the sky in the east held the promise of a sunny day. The sun had yet to come up, but it appeared as though the sky would be cloudless, soon to turn bright blue with a light breeze. It would be a perfect day to walk out of the woods and start my drive south.

I hung around Cedar Lakes until around 10:00 A.M. before saddling up and commencing the hike to Perkins Clearing. The full week of rain had wreaked havoc on the trails, which for most of the walk were completely submerged. I truly looked forward to getting back to my rusty old jalopy, where I knew I'd find a fresh set of socks and my dry pair of work shoes.

Following the pattern of the past three days, I saw absolutely no one on the trails until I made it past Sled Harbor and then onto the main logging road. I was passing the old lean-to by the bridge over the Miami River[2] when I noticed a couple of elderly folks sitting inside.

I sauntered up the few feet of ground to the front of the lean-to and raised a hand of greeting.

"Well, hello!" I said, looking between the man and the woman, both of whom appeared to be in their mid-to-late seventies. "I don't see people at this lean-to very often. It looks like you've got quite a spread set out for yourself."

"Yes, yes, we enjoy coming back in here every once in a while," smiled the man. "We used to do quite a bit of this kind of thing, but we're not really as active as we once were, so this is nice."

I looked down at the feast that was laid out on the wooden floor of the lean-to, neatly arranged on the red and white plaid tablecloth. There were sandwiches, rolls, drinks, and even some small containers with side dishes to complement the main meal. All it needed was a candelabra to resemble the dining room of a fancy restaurant. I was impressed.

"Well, you've sure put my food pack to shame," I said, looking from one dish to another. "I eat almost anything I can catch, or meals that require no more than one cooking step...as in 'add boiling water and stir!'"

They both got a laugh out of that one.

[2] This lean-to has been gone for many years, and not even a trace of it remains today. It was not officially inside the West Canada Lakes Wilderness Area, but I considered it to be part of my patrol as I had to walk past it each time I came in via the Perkins Clearing route.

"Well, this is something of a special event for us," said the man. This is the fifty-fifth anniversary of our wedding day, and we wanted to do something unusual. We're going out with our children and grandchildren later on today, but this lunch was just for us. Martha and I used to love coming up here from Gloversville. We'd camp for a week at a time and roam all over the woods together. But like I said, we can't do that anymore, so this is our campout for the year."

As he spoke, he looked at his bride of over half a century, and the two of them touched hands. It was, I thought, a very simple motion that spoke volumes.

"You know, it's really amazing," I said, "but I camped next to a couple of folks from southern New York this week who were actually on their honeymoon! So meeting you today, celebrating your anniversary, is quite the coincidence."

"Yes, I imagine it is" said the woman, who had remained quiet up to this point. "And were they enjoying themselves back there?"

"Well, yes, they seemed quite happy together, although they did do a bit of quarreling for a pair that was just hitched."

"Quarreling?" the woman repeated, her head tilted in a way that demanded more information.

"Oh, you know, simple things, like who should have packed what," I replied. "Nothing really serious."

"Oh my God" said the elderly gentleman, tipping his head back in laughter. "They'd better get used to it. That never goes away. Ever!" He laughed some more and appeared to be enjoying the image of the bickering newlyweds. "But you know what? Over time, you just sort of tune that stuff out. I learned long ago that I'm always wrong and Martha is always right. Even when I'm right, I'm wrong. Right honey?" He looked again at his wife as he spoke.

"Yes, dear, that's right," she replied, touching him again on the shoulder. "Either that or he just turns off his hearing aid." Again, another round of laughter, accompanied by more romantic glances. It was heartwarming to see, and I quickly decided to

24

leave this couple to themselves so that they might enjoy the rest of their celebratory meal in private.

As I walked the remaining mile out to my car, I thought about what I'd seen that week. Two couples, on the opposite ends of life, yet both filled with passion toward their partners. Separated by a mere fifty-five years of marriage, they both enjoyed each other as they enjoyed their surroundings. Together, these two couples represented a pair of bookends, of a sort, living proof that love can prosper and grow over the expanse of time. Although I was not yet married myself, I hoped that someday I would be able to enjoy that same kind of relationship, with or without a hearing aid.

—4—

Match Point

It was a most unusual sight. Actually, I heard it long before I saw it—the turbo-powered sound of an Olympic swim meet as powerful legs and arms thrust their way across the water. It sounded distant but very powerful.

As I cleared the last stand of trees and emerged into the clearing that surrounded the lean-to at Cedar Lakes Dam, I saw the source of the sound. It was a swimmer—no, two swimmers—locked in a head-to-head race across the narrow end of the lake. Adding even more volume to the noise was a large golden retriever, who seemed to be content with riding the wake of these two aquatic stars as they stroked their way through the shining waters. Near the other side floated a bright pink Frisbee, which seemed to be the destination of all three bodies in the water.

From the trail, I caught a glimpse of two healthy-looking young women standing in front of the lean-to, alternately cheering and bursting out in hysterics. They were obviously all part of the same group, although there was a definite competitive division between the couples.

"Hey there!" I called out, not wanting to startle anyone

(least of all the dog) by my appearance. "I guess they forgot to tell me about the Cedar Lakes Swim Meet today!"

"Oh, God, no!" one of the women replied. "It's bad enough they have to make fools of themselves when no one else is around. Now we've got the ranger involved. We're not going to jail, are we?" This set off yet another round of laughter.

"No, not at all," I said. "But I've got to admit, this is the first time I've ever seen anything like this. Are they competitive swimmers?"

The other woman, who was shorter than her companion, with wavy brown hair, answered quickly. "Competitive, yes. Swimmers, no. But it really doesn't matter what sport you choose. Those two will compete for stakes in tiddlywinks if you let them. They're hopeless!"

By now, the two men were stroking their way slowly back across to our side of the lake. The dog, who had been carrying the Frisbee in its mouth, suddenly caught sight of me and decided that I was a threat. It dropped the Frisbee and commenced a series of warning barks, although they didn't seem terribly serious considering that the dog was still paddling madly just trying to reach the shore.

I must admit that, at times like this, I did feel a certain bit of tension, as most animals tend to become a little territorial in the woods. Additionally, there were some dogs that just did not like people in uniform. I had heard of countless mail carriers who were attacked by canines that were usually quite docile. I knew that most retrievers are friendly, affectionate animals, but I didn't want to be on the wrong end of a sharp set of incisors.

"He is friendly, I hope?" I asked the taller of the two women.

"Oh yes, he's just got a loud bark. Don't let that scare you. He'll probably just lick you to death."

"What's his name?" I asked, wanting to be able to give him a familiar greeting once he made his final charge. He was now within a few feet of the shore, and his feet were touching the bottom.

"Spot," was the answer. It was said quickly, with no trace of humor.

"Spot," I echoed. "You are kidding, right"

"Yes, Spot. It was my husband's idea," she said, rolling her eyes skyward. "And if we had a cat, he'd have named her Puff. I guarantee it." That set her friend off into another fit of giggles.

By now, Spot was on the shore, barking and charging up the bank. He hadn't bothered shaking the water out of his coat, being too preoccupied with me as a newcomer to the scene. However, I had little to worry about. Instead of aggression, Spot came dancing over in a rapid series of gyrating jumps and capers that sent tiny jets of water flying in assorted directions, including my own. His lolling tongue made a few attempts at wetting my raised hands, indicating his obvious good nature.

As the two men emerged from the water, Spot decided that he should have a proper shake-down. He went into one of those full-body quivering motions that started up by his head and increased in intensity until the entire dog was wrapped up in it, whirling and wringing and flinging every drop of water out of his massively dense coat. The terminal phase involved a final whipping of the tail, which by itself proved to hold a surprising quantity of water.

I was soaked. Had I known that this was coming, I wouldn't have bothered bathing the previous evening in West Canada Creek. Even when submerged in the rapidly flowing waters of the stream, I could hardly have been more saturated with water than I was now.

"Spot, NO!!! STOP THAT!" called one of the women, trying to grab onto part of the animal that was still in the spin-dry cycle. Even the two men, who were dressed in only their swim trunks, stepped back involuntarily. They acted embarrassed at my now-drenched uniform.

"Oh, that's OK," I said, trying to make the best of it. It's a hot day, and I'm pretty soaked from my own sweat anyway. To

28

tell you the truth, it feels kind of good."

The two men quickly introduced themselves as Keith and Lou. Keith was a tall, blond-haired fellow with blue eyes and wide shoulders. He looked very much the athlete. Lou was shorter and a bit on the stockier side. They also introduced me to their spouses, both of whom were named Sue. The taller of the two, though, pointed out that she went by Susan, not Sue. She was married to Keith, while the shorter Sue was Lou's wife.

This foursome had never visited the West Canadas, but they'd heard about the area from a good friend. They had opted for the shortest route in, via Perkins Clearing, rather than try to cover any distance of the Northville-Lake Placid Trail.

As Keith and Lou dried off and changed into their clothes, Susan filled me in on their choice of hiking destinations. "Oh, we're not really very ambitious," she said, her long blonde hair blowing in the warm breeze. "As a matter of fact, most of the time we just get a campsite at one of the campgrounds and spend our days lazing around the lake. This is really much different for us."

As I sat down on the front log of the lean-to, I listened to the foursome talk about life back home in Syracuse, not far from where I had recently attended school. Both Keith and Lou were teachers in the city school system, where they had met and become friends some time ago. Since that time, they had apparently discovered a mutual love for sports competition. They were teammates on city basketball and softball teams, and they were also involved in a number of other sports on a less organized basis.

My route that week would have me camping at Cedar Lakes the next two nights, as I was to make my weekly day trek up and back to Cedar River Flow the next day before leaving the woods on Tuesday afternoon. I quickly decided to set up my tent near the lean-to, in the hope that my new friends would keep an eye on my equipment.

"Sure, we'd love to," said Lou when I posed the question.

"We're not going anywhere until Wednesday afternoon, so we'd gladly watch your stuff. It will be guarded by Spot, the fearless attack watch dog! Nothing will ever disappear while he's on the job!"

The remark drew a round of laughter from the friends, which further confirmed my assumption that the retriever was completely friendly. Spot, however, seemed to know that he was the topic of discussion, as he sat up and let loose a single "Woof!" More laughter.

Before setting out to check the area, as I often did in mid-afternoon, I decided to have a bite to eat. I loosened the drawstrings on my pack and extracted the ingredients for one of my gourmet peanut butter and jelly sandwiches. (It was gourmet because I was using an expensive jar of brand-name jelly that week instead of the cheap dollar store variety!) As I started cutting two slices from the thick loaf of rye, I noticed that I had company. Spot's nose repeatedly intruded into my corner of the lean-to; he was obviously eager to find out just how easy a mark I would be. I broke down and handed him a chunk of the bread, which he devoured quickly before returning his steady gaze in my direction.

As I started consuming my sandwich, the rest of the campers began cleaning up their leftover dishes and scraps from their late breakfast. I watched as Keith squashed a large piece of aluminum foil into a little round ball. He then gracefully extended a long arm over his head and cut loose with an impressive basketball hook shot, sending the tin foil ball arcing into an empty coffee can on the other side of the lean-to.

"Yes," he called out, pumping his first as though he'd just made the clinching three-pointer in an NBA playoff game. "This kid is good! Let's see you try that one, Bucky!" (From the way that the remark was made, I took it that "Bucky" was a nickname that was not equally espoused by Lou.)

Lou, who had been watching from the camp table, couldn't

30

resist. "I'll make that shot twice for every one that you can put in, chump!"

Keith giggled, the women rolled their eyes, Spot barked, and another impromptu sports dual was on. Keith and Lou placed the coffee can squarely in the middle of the lean-to and set about a woodsy game of basketball. Unfortunately for Susan and Sue, that left the rest of the clean-up for them alone, which they seemed to accept as normal. I decided to stay out of it and start my inspection around the near-by tent sites. As I left the premises, I heard a running commentary breaking out about the ease or difficulty of the shots as they were attempted. The score was tied as I headed away from the lean-to.

As I strolled around the east end of Cedar Lakes, I poked around several tent sites that I seldom visited. I was always interested to see the places that people decided to set up tents and campsites, especially during those few times when the woods were truly full and they were forced away from the lean-tos. Some tent sites were situated in wonderful locations with flat ground and soft soil, while others had been placed in clearings that were crisscrossed with semi-submerged roots. These roots often rose several inches above the ground, and in some cases were quite knobby. Whoever placed their sleeping bags here must have had either very thick foam pads or a wonderful ability to withstand pain. Ouch!

From the tent sites, I wandered down Cedar River, stepping over the stones below the dam and following the river's course north-ward. Here were several of my favorite fishing holes, quiet little eddies off of the main current. I often stopped here to see whether I could pull in a small "sandwich trout" for my evening meal.

By the time I made it back to the lean-to, it was late afternoon, and the women were already thinking about making preparations for an early supper. The men weren't involved in this process, nor could they have been. They appeared to be wrapped up in a life-or-death struggle for the goal line. As I watched in amusement (and some degree of horror), the two men engaged in a truly hard-hitting match of one-on-one football. The ball was a small, squeezable plastic football with a simulated "pigskin" cover. It could be squashed down to a very small size, which is how Keith and Lou seemed to carry it while protecting it from one another.

"Ugh...aghhh!" screamed Lou as he put his head into Keith's stomach. Keith responded by putting an elbow on top of Lou's head, sending him crashing to the ground on top of an old tree stump.

"Later, Bucky!" yelled Keith, as he prepared to dart off towards the imaginary goal line, which was some undefined point near the water. Unfortunately, that was as far as he got before Lou reached up and snagged his sneakered foot, sending the now off-balanced Keith reeling headfirst into the shallow water. Lou had a scraped shoulder, Keith's clothes were soaked, and Spot was barking in a not-so-friendly way. Yet the two men were laughing as they got up to start another series of plays.

I had seen campers bring in Frisbees and other play things in the past, although I couldn't understand the need. I loved just sitting and observing all the wildlife around me and taking in the outrageous sunsets each evening. But Keith and Lou seemed to have a virtual sporting goods store with them. I had already seen Frisbees, a football, a tennis ball, and a few toys meant solely for the dog. I wondered what other surprises were still in their packs, waiting to be revealed. I could hardly wait.

I thought about saying something when the football game turned rough, although I held my thoughts to myself. After all, there was no rule against full contact tackle football in the woods, although it would be me who ended up escorting (translate to "carrying") any injured contestants back to Perkins Clearing. That wouldn't be pretty. I need not have worried, though, as the game ended fairly soon with the announcement of dinner. The wounds were quickly dressed and the evening took on a peaceful tone. Perhaps I should call it a ceasefire.

Over dinner, we had another very enjoyable conversation,

with the four campers asking me about my work arrangement with the state. This was always a topic of discussion in the woods, where we really couldn't go "off duty" no matter what time of day it was.

"You mean, you only get paid for a forty-hour week?" asked Keith, staring through wide-open eyes. "It's not like you can go home at the end of the day and be with your family. I'd think that they'd find a way to do more than that for you, like an extra day off each week, or something."

"Oh, it's really not bad," I countered. "I get Wednesday and Thursday off, and I leave the woods at a fairly decent hour on Tuesday. Plus, just think about it: how many times have you decided to go camping on your days off back home, only to have something get in the way? Well, I get to go every week, rain or shine...whether I want to or not!"

This drew a bit of laughter from my new friends. "I bet there are some times when you're just not up to it," asked Susan. "Like when it's raining cats and dogs?"

"Or when some camper's golden retriever shakes seventy pounds of doggy water all over your nice, clean uniform," added Sue. Everyone looked towards the canine for another vocal reaction. However, he was already paying attention to the contents of the cook pot and couldn't be bothered with a response.

The few clouds that had formed a tapestry across the skies cleared out after dinner, and the sun turned the western sky a deepening hue of orange. This was when, on certain special nights, the breeze died off completely and the trout rose up in numbers near the dam. I decided to try my luck out with a worm and a few casts.

As I have often said, I am an extremely unskilled fisherman, and my sole talent extends only as far as threading an unfortunate worm onto a hook. However, on this evening, that was all it took. On only my third or fourth cast, I felt a distinct tug, which caused me to tug back and successfully set the hook. As the tension on the line increased, I felt the excitement of the ensuing fight, as well as the anticipation of treating myself to another course for my evening meal. It felt like a substantial fish.

Although I remained fairly silent, my activities aroused the curiosity of Keith and Lou, who were at my side in a moment. Spot, too, was highly interested and joined us at the water's edge. It was a fairly short battle of about three or four minutes before I was able to tire the fish and land him safely in the grass beside the water. It was a nice looking brook trout, not overly long, perhaps about eleven to twelve inches, but beautifully speckled along its underbelly. I was quite pleased with myself.

That was all it took to start Round #4. Keith looked at Lou. Lou looked at Keith. And they both disappeared in a mad dash back to the lean-to, trying to be the first one among them to land the next fish. Their fishing gear must have been buried quite deeply in their packs, for I had a quick glimpse of various pieces of equipment and clothing flying in all directions as the two raced to assemble their rods and tackle. The two women ignored them entirely, instead deciding to enjoy their conversation over the remains of the cooking fire. They were used to the competitions by now.

I broke out my frying pan and created a truly sumptuous version of Larry's Trout in Olive Oil and Bread Crumbs. I really didn't need this extra course, as I was fairly full from the meal I had just consumed. However, I loved trout, and I always had a hard time turning down a good fish once one came my way. As I cooked, Keith and Lou were frantically casting their lines, jockeying with one another for the best spot on the shore. Prior to this, I had never seen a hip check employed in the sport of trout fishing. To tell the truth, I'm a bit surprised that one of them didn't end up snagging the other while casting. But they didn't, although neither of them was lucky enough to duplicate my catch. (No wonder; every trout in Hamilton County had probably heard the commotion and evacuated the region for quieter waters!)

Tuesday morning dawned with the promise of another beautiful day. There wasn't a cloud in sight, and the moderate tempera-ture was indicative of a day that would be not too hot, not too cool. This would be perfect weather for my hike down and back to the lean-to at Cedar River Flow. It was an easy route, about ten to eleven miles on good trail. The lean-to there was very seldom used, as the "through hikers" who hiked the entire Northville-Placid Trail tended to go from Wakely Dam all the way to Cedar Lakes in a single shot.

Because my day's hike would be an easy one, and I had the benefit of being able to leave my large pack and most of its weight behind, I decided to put off leaving until mid-morning. Even with a lengthy stop at the other end, I knew I'd be back by early afternoon, so there was no need to rush. I went around to the back of the lean-to with the idea of getting rid of some of the oversized plastic sheets I'd seen on the ground the previous evening. (Winter campers often brought these in to seal off the snow and high winds in the colder weather; however, they very seldom had the consideration to carry them back out of the woods.) As I folded the heavy material and commenced pushing it under the lean-to, I heard the distinct sound of a knife hitting wood. With a dull "TWANG," the steel bit into the bottom boards of the lean-to.

Knife throwing? Was there no end to the competitions? The repeated sound of the blade hitting the wood was accompanied by high pitched squeals of laughter, which for reasons I could not gather were increasing in volume with each successive strike.

Suddenly, from out of nowhere, I heard the unspeakable: "Oh, man, you've put the blade right through my toe!"

What? With speed worthy of an NFL linebacker, I dashed around to the front of the lean-to, ready to fly into action and apply direct pressure somewhere. However, much to my relief, all I saw was Lou, holding up an empty boot that was now perfo-rated with a single knife slit. Evidently, they had been playing a competitive round of "mumblety-pegs," but at least had dis-played the common sense to aim at an empty pair of footwear. With a waning smile on my face, I retreated towards my tent, intent on starting my hike without further delay.

The remainder of the day was quiet, and my hike to and from the Cedar River Flow was uneventful. I spent longer than usual at the northern end of my route that day, and I even covered some of the distance between the Flow and Wakely Dam. This wasn't part of my assigned route, and for that matter wasn't even part of Tom Eakin's territory. However, it was pretty country, and I sometimes enjoyed the longer strolls with only my day pack.

It was fairly late in the day by the time I arrived back at the dam. My presence was duly noted by Spot, who barked his greet-ings from a distance of several hundred feet. No bears would be seen around our neck of the woods tonight. As I would be leav-ing the woods the next morning for my days off, I shared a few more of my leftovers with the friendly retriever. He had long since become accustomed to my bits of pepperoni and bread, tossed his way before and after the evening meal.

"I think he'll miss you when you leave tomorrow," said Susan, as she ran her hands through his mane of golden locks. "We try to watch what we give him, but he's found a willing donor since you arrived."

"I can't help it," I replied. "I grew up with a Lab as a boy, so I've always been partial to retrievers. They're just such fantas-tic animals."

"Well, he's really enjoyed himself back here. And as long as he can carry his own doggy pack, it's been no extra work for us. As long as he doesn't get lost on the walk out of here tomorrow."

That last remark puzzled me somewhat, so I had to inquire. "What do you mean 'get lost'? He'll just walk along with you, won't he?"

"Oh, no," was the response from Susan, although she drew out her words as though something was definitely not right.

"We're not walking out as a group. Keith and Lou got into a debate yesterday about who hikes faster, so they're having a walk-race to see who makes it back to the van first."

"You've got to be kidding me!" I replied, casting a sideways glance at Keith. He was standing out by the table, sheepishly looking back at me while shrugging his shoulders.

"What can I say," he said, the ever widening grin splitting his face. "Bucky here challenged me to a race, and it's for the first round of beers when we hit town on Wednesday. I'm not about to back down from a free round of brew!"

"You gotta be kidding me," said Lou. "You'll be eating my dust by the time we hit the one-mile marker. After that, you won't see me again until you get to Perkins Clearing!"

The women had been right from the start; these two were hopeless. It didn't matter what sport, or event, or even the hike out of the woods. They were going to compete in everything.

Even though their spouses were enjoying themselves to the max, I wanted to make certain that Sue and Susan would be able to find their own way out of the woods on their own. (Who had the map, anyway?)

Susan quickly put my mind at ease about that matter. "Oh, it's OK. It's really a pretty simple route, and we saw the trail signs the whole way in. Besides, Spot will be with us, and he'll be able to tell which way the guys went."

It wasn't a perfect answer, and I must admit that I disagreed with the two men leaving their partners behind as they raced to the finish line. But they were all adults, and there was nothing illegal about the activity. Just a little bit strange, that's all.

I never saw any of them again, as it was another three weeks before I returned and inspected the Perkins Clearing register booth. Curious about the final sign-out, I turned the register back a number of pages until I arrived at the day of their departure. Sure enough, on the original line where the four of them had signed in, I saw the customary single word, "Out," scrawled next to Sue, Susan, and Keith. However, at the bottom of that same page was a departure note left by Lou. It read "Lou—Syracuse, NY, Wednesday, 1:21 P.M. Keith—eat my dust!"

Spot never bothered signing out.

—5—

The Bear Truth

It was the nicest of days, perhaps seventy degrees, with very low humidity. The sky was an unbroken blanket of dark blue, and a light breeze was fanning the carpet of ferns that covered the forest floor. Not a mosquito was to be seen anywhere, and I was bounding merrily up the dirt road that ascended Blue Ridge (or what some local hikers affectionately nicknamed "sonofabitch hill").

As I crested the top of the rise, my eyes automatically went into telephoto zoom mode, looking ahead towards the long row of raspberry bushes which lined the path as it started its descent towards Grassy Brook. These bushes had been growing and spreading for years and often contained enough ripe fruit to make a fair-sized lunch. I had passed that way a week earlier and noticed that the crop was coming along quite nicely; it was now just about ready to pick.

I sauntered down the middle of the road (which used to be a jeep trail for getting in to some hunting camps), all the while scanning the bushes. Yes, it did look like a very good year. The berries were above average in size and held a deep red color. Several of the nearby branches were positively loaded, bowing slightly under the weight of the ripe fruit. I slipped my pack off in anticipation, propping it upright in the road with my walking stick. This would be great!

Before starting my feast, I removed the canteen from my belt and took a long drink. The walk up the ridge always made me thirsty, and I closed my eyes as I swallowed the cool water in big gulps. Consuming at least half of the container, I reopened my eyes to screw the cap back on the canteen.

Hello!

I stopped in mid-turn as I saw her standing there, perhaps sixty feet away. She looked like the biggest bear in the world, even though I realized that she probably only weighed a couple hundred pounds. Funny as it sounds, bears always look a lot larger if they are not fenced in. And the closer you get to an uncontained bear, the bigger they appear to be!

Anyway, this one was sitting in the middle of the raspberry patch, licking her chops appreciatively. I wasn't sure about this, but I thought I heard a soft grunting sound coming from her throat as she consumed the berries, often pulling off sections of branches as she ate.

Seeing me approach, she went up on her hind legs, which elevated her head to a height of perhaps five or six feet. She pointed her nose up in the air, sniffing out my scent while looking at my stationary form. Having decided that I was probably not a threat, she came back down onto all fours and resumed her foraging. However, before she did, she gave me a long appraising stare that was very clear in its intent.

It was almost as though the bear was saying, "Look, pal, I was here first, and these are my berries. I'm the bear, and you're not, so you'd better stay clear of me. OK?"

OK. I could live with that. I picked up my pack and moved it back up the trail about a hundred yards, deciding to watch the bear as it moved from bush to bush. For animals that have a reputation for being clumsy, they can actually be quite graceful.

I removed the microphone of my radio from the side pocket of my pack and turned to face the Pillsbury Mountain fire tower. The trail up Blue Ridge runs directly past the trailhead for the tower, and I knew that I'd be able to make radio contact from this location. It was one of the few spots that was actually reliable in our area, as most of the time I was incommunicado.

"Pillsbury, this is 1051," I called out, identifying myself by my radio number. The response was almost instantaneous.

"1051, this is Pillsbury Mountain, roger, over." It was a female voice, since John Remias' daughter Marion was staffing the tower that summer.

"Pillsbury, this is 1051. I'm going to be going out of service here for a short while, Marion. I'm trying to get by the Pillsbury Lake junction on the road down here, but there's a really cute looking momma bear who's threatening to rearrange my body if I come too much closer. So I'm just going to relax here for a while until she eats her fill, and then I'll get going again."

I could here Marion chuckling to herself as she tried to speak. "OK, now," she advised me. "Don't get into any trouble, or I'll have to send Scamp down to rescue you." Scamp was the Remias' old hound dog who accompanied Marion up the mountain every week. He made for loyal company, and he also served as watchdog of the Pillsbury fire tower cabin.

"Roger that," I replied quickly. "I don't think there's any need, though. Our only disagreement is that we've both apparently been scouting out the same berry patch. I think she won."

Marion laughed in agreement, then signed off to go down to her cabin for lunch. She promised me, though, that she'd bring the radio down with her, in case I needed help. Thankfully, I was sure I wouldn't require any assistance, because I knew that the bear would pretty much ignore me if I just kept my distance.

I waited for an additional ten or fifteen minutes as the hungry animal completed her meal, after which she departed through the back of the patch and moved through the trees towards the side of Page Mountain. I knew that there would still be a good supply of berries left, since bears aren't known for being the world's greatest searchers. They tend to eat what's visible near the tops and sides of the bushes and don't bother much with what's buried inside the middle of the plants.

From watching this particular bear, I could tell that she had probably grown up on the outskirts of civilization, most likely near roads and camping facilities. The reason she didn't run when I appeared was that she had seen humans before. However, she wasn't as familiar with people as some of her relatives who hang around the village dumps or visit the campsites inside the state campgrounds. Those animals can truly be a nuisance, and they occasionally have to be dealt with.

In many ways, it's not the bears' fault; they have been trained to bother people. It is a common sight at many of the camp-grounds run by the state to see campers approaching these huge animals with slices of bread and sandwich meat, all the while the rest of the family is snapping photographs in the background. And, while this may make a wonderful addition to the "What I did on my summer vacation" scrapbook, it is far from being a pru-dent thing to do. These animals are extremely powerful and can run at a speed that far exceeds that of their human counterparts.

Not that the black bears living in the Adirondacks are dangerous when compared to, say, the grizzly bears found in the western United States; they're not. They are much more docile and gen-erally won't attack unless they're protecting their young, or when they're severely provoked. But, as with any wild animal, it's better to be safe than sorry. I always tried to give them a rather large amount of leeway whenever encountering bears on the trail.

Whenever I was asked about the difference between a black bear and a grizzly, I always responded with a favorite line, which I had heard spoken by a park ranger in Yellowstone National Park. With a bit of a smile, she responded to the question by saying,

"Well, it's easy to tell them apart. Whenever you're being chased by a bear, just climb up the nearest tree you can find. If the bear climbs up the tree after you, it's a black bear. If it just pulls the tree out by its roots, it's a grizzly!" I used that line extensively, and it usually drew a round of nervous laughter from my audience.

In general, most of the folks hiking far back into the woods weren't really worried about running into bears. I'd occasionally meet up with a gun-toting warrior who was convinced that the best way to keep a campsite safe was to throw out a continuous stream of gunfire into the woods in all directions. Most of these folks tended to be on the lower end of the experience scale, though, and I tried to give them even more leeway than I gave the bears. After all, I'd never seen a bear with a high powered rifle before. (And even if I had, I doubt that he would have been able to purchase enough ammunition to keep the gun loaded for long!)

The small groups of Boy Scouts who passed through from time to time always asked a lot of bear questions. Usually, these wide-eyed youngsters, perhaps ten or twelve years of age, displayed a unique range of emotions whenever I mentioned the bears in the area. From their expressions, I could see that they were quite afraid of the beasts, but they still wanted to see one while they were back there, just to tell their friends about it.

For these fledgling woodsmen, I'd go through my standard bear story, adding more details with each subsequent telling of the tale. I'd try to start it out realistically, by saying that, "A bear came past my tent just the other night. I could hear him, just on the other side of the tent flap, as he sniffed around for food."

As the eyes of the boys widened in surprise, I'd add that, "The bear suddenly swiped a paw under the front of the tent, pulling me right out of my sleeping bag. So I got up and swung as hard as I could, punching him in the nose. Then, he gave me a bear hug, so I bit his ear, and he swiped my jaw, and...," all the while doing my best to animate the imaginary battle with quick jabs and head movements.

By this time, the Scouts were usually all giggling merrily, happy to learn that bears didn't really drag people out of their tents. It was a popular routine, and several groups asked me to provide encore appearances of my act. I soon considered it to be part of my duties to have a large collection of bear stories, and I got quite good at telling them.

As I said, most of the people passing through our territory, including the Boy Scouts, did look forward to seeing at least one of these critters during their stay in the woods. I think that many of them would have been disappointed if they had known that the bears living deep in the woods are very seldom seen. It's not unusual to come across their tracks, especially after it's rained and the ground is soft. Their droppings are also frequent sights along the trails, as are scratch marks on trees as they dig their sharp claws into the soft bark. But "wilderness" bears were much harder to come across than their suburban counterparts. They do live there, and in fact thrive in such settings. However, they are just not used to seeing people and will generally move in the other direction when they sense one coming.

One lesson that I learned the hard way was that a bear, when stationary, can blend in quite well with its surroundings. I was coming along the north side of Cedar Lakes one evening, returning to my lean-to after stopping by to check on a group that was staying at the Beaver Pond. It was around eight o'clock, and the woods were basked in the golden light that signifies the sun going down near the horizon. It was a lovely evening, and I moved along the trail quickly since I was not carrying a pack.

As I crested the land on the east side of the pond outlet, I was startled by the sound of pounding feet and crashing bushes. I had unknowingly come upon a good-sized bear, which had probably been watching me from behind a patch of dense brush, remaining concealed until I approached too close for his comfort. Once I was within about one hundred feet of his hiding spot, he took off with a quickness and speed that stunned me. About all I saw of the large animal was the sunlight reflecting off his coat as he streaked away from the trail. As he went, he literally bent over saplings that were approximately one inch in diameter.

It was an awesome sight, and I'd be lying if I said that I wasn't a bit spooked by the episode. As I stood there watching the rapidly fleeing animal, I could hear my heart pounding away inside my chest. I believe that's called the "fight or flight" reaction, although I'm sure that neither of those actions would have helped me in that situation. My only saving grace was that the bear seemed to be even more afraid of me than I was of him.

By coincidence, the only other close call (if that's what it must be called) that I had in my tenure in the West Canadas took place within a few hundred yards of the first saga. Once again, I was on the east side of the Beaver Pond, although I had barely walked over the bridge, and was moving along the sandy stretch of trail that hugs the shore of the lake. I had covered about fifty yards, moving towards the same hill, when a fairly small bear, probably a yearling, popped out of the dense spruce thicket and onto the trail, perhaps fifty yards ahead of me. It spotted me and turned to face me. However, it did not run. (Perhaps it wanted to see what a human looked like!)

Deciding that I had already seen a bear, and that I wasn't particularly in the mood to see another, I turned around and started walking in the other direction. I didn't run, as I didn't want to trigger a chase reaction from the bear. Instead, I opted for a slow and deliberate retreat.

As I started those first few steps back towards the bridge, something genuinely scary happened; another bear, which strongly resembled the first one in every way, including size, appeared from the trees on the other side of me. I was now surrounded! And it, like its companion in back of me, did not seem intimidated. It, too, stood its ground and looked at me.

With no place to go but the water, I slowly unbuckled the hip strap on my pack and began backing into the brush that rimmed the lake. If these two "youngsters" decided that they wanted to play, I was going to have to get wet. I only hoped that it wouldn't come to that, as I really didn't feel like ditching my pack and going for a fully-dressed swim.

The two bears, which were probably siblings, watched me from the trail for a short while. (It may have been only a few seconds; time seemed to be standing still as I hastily planned my escape.) Then, as if on cue, they both turned north and headed back into the woods above the trail. I stood there watching them for a few minutes as they pushed their way through the conifers, finally disappearing from sight.

Thank heavens that confrontations such as that occurred extremely infrequently in my territory, even around campsites, whereas most hikers who have been through the more populated areas (such as the High Peaks) are used to seeing a more "friendly" variety of the species on a regular basis. These amiable members of the black bear family enjoy stopping by campsites to investigate the many smells and tastes that rise from the lean-to cooking grates. While these animals are great for providing memorable snapshots, I never missed their presence in the West Canadas.

As a matter of fact, because of their reclusive nature in our territory, I was able to avoid one of the Adirondack hiker's daily rituals, which is the solemn "hanging of the food bag" before turning in at night. (In many areas, this has been replaced by mandatory bear-proof food containers.) Not once in three years did I have to do this, which is something that I was constantly thankful for. Many of my colleagues in other areas had to become quite skilled at this chore, and I marveled at the heights at which their caches had to be stowed.

One gentleman I encountered at South Lake informed me that he usually tried to get his food bag at least twenty-five feet off the ground and a minimum of twenty feet from the nearest tree limb. When he asked me where I'd recommend hanging his sack for the night, he acted shocked when I pointed at a nail on the side of the lean-to and said "that ought to do it." The white-haired hiker, who was one of the only senior citizens I had ever met hiking the trail alone, looked at me incredulously.

"No, you're kidding?" he asked, tilting his head to one side. "Where I come from, I wouldn't have any food left in the morning if I did that. Are you sure?"

I nodded and pointed to my own green bag, which was hanging securely from its own nail over my sleeping bag. "Yup, that's all you've got to do back here. The only threat to your food in this lean-to is from me; I tend to get hungry in the middle of the night, so I grab whatever's handy. You got anything good in there?"

He laughed and took me at my word, hanging his food on a nail adjacent to mine.

In a way, I could understand his hesitation; I had been quite doubtful when hunters told me during my first weeks in the woods that I didn't need to take such precautions. I believed them, although I was a bit nervous for the first month or so, until I realized that we just didn't have a problem in the West Canada Lakes. (Either that, or bears didn't care for my cooking enough to stop by for a sample.)

Adding to my initial worries were the graffiti inscriptions about bear encounters, carved and written into the lean-tos by hundreds of visitors over the years. For the most part, they were comical to the point of disbelief, so I read them as pure fiction. However, some of them were more believable, which lead me to think that at various times over the years, bears had been more of a nuisance than they were while I was working there.

Personally, I enjoyed the more unusual entries, many of which had been written ten and twenty years in the past. Several of them took advantage of famous quotes, such as: "Mike shot a bear in his pajamas; how it got in his pajamas I'll never know," referring to the famous Marx Brothers movie.

Another one, written into the original lean-to by the dam at

Cedar Lakes, described the adventures of one particularly savvy fishing group, stating that a bear had come after the thousands of trout they had caught, but that "John chased it away with his machete." Wow. John must have been a brave man!

All in all, though, I had it relatively easy. The number of bear encounters I had while living on the trail could be counted on my fingers and toes, with only a few really harrowing experiences. That is, of course, except for the time that a bear suddenly swiped a paw under the front of my tent, pulling me right out of my sleeping bag.

Perhaps I should tell you about it.

—6—

That Cursed Paperwork

It had to be the hottest day of the year, at least 105 degrees in the shade. And I wasn't sitting in the shade. No, I was working at the makeshift table in front of the southern-most lean-to on Spruce Lake, trying to figure out just what it was that I was supposed to write down on this confounded form. It was part of my job, part of the paperwork assigned to the wilderness park ranger position, and I didn't enjoy it.

Staring blankly at the surveys, the questions danced in circles before my eyes. Nothing was really clear. Did the "numbers of groups encountered" include individuals, or not? (Is one person a group?) And how about the section that asked for "number of nights spent in campsite"—did that mean in all of the campsites during a single groups' hike through the area, or was that to specify the number of nights at a single campsite? The number of combinations was virtually endless.

I pondered the questions for quite a while, doing my best to answer them honestly and accurately. But after a good half hour of this mental gridlock, I took the piece of paper, which was by then filled with crossed-out figures and inscriptions, and applied my lighter to its corner.

Aha! Now that's how to dispose of paperwork! What a great way to get a fire going in ultra-rainy weather! Within a minute, however, I was feeling guilty and extracted a new form from my pack in order to make a fresh attempt.

You see, I've never been what you'd call a top-notch administrator. As a matter of fact, I'm pretty lousy at the entire process of report-submitting and paper-filing. I'm not really certain whether it's a lack of application on my part, or perhaps the result of a genetic defect. But the end result has always been the same—massive and ultimate administrative bedlam.

One quick look at my desk when I was in college would have been enough to confirm this assessment. While I admire people who can leave work at the end of the day with a completely clean desktop, mine is usually hidden underneath six to eight inches of old (and usually outdated) garbage. I'm a one-man administrative nightmare, a walking paperwork black-hole into which papers disappear, never to be seen again.

But none of that mattered anymore. Right?

Before ever reporting to the job that first year, I remember painting an image of a job that was totally free of forms, papers, and offices. It would be just me and my pack, tromping around miles of administrative-free trails without a care in the world. After all, why would anyone carry paperwork into the woods with them, unless they intended to use it as kindling on very wet days?

Until I started working for the state that first summer, my only experience with "backcountry paperwork" was encountered one rainy afternoon as I was hiking in the High Peaks Region, as I was making my way around the rocky shoreline of Avalanche Lake. On the trail ahead, I spotted two innocent-looking individuals with clipboards in their hands. (This is not normal behavior, and I immediately suspected that something was up!) As I approached, one of the gentlemen identified himself as a student from a local forestry school and asked me if I'd take a survey to assist them in their studies of land use.

What? This was impossible! This was just the kind of thing that I'd come up here to get away from. It just wasn't fair. However, trying my best to be a good citizen, I accepted the form and sat down on a rock to provide my input.

As I looked at the document, another hiker appeared on the well-used trail and diverted the attention of the survey takers. And while they addressed him, I quickly turned the page and got a sneak preview of the questions on page two. And then on page three. And then pages four, five, and six! This wasn't a survey; it was a final exam! Perhaps they wanted me to write a term paper while I was at it.

It was about that time that I flipped back to the first page and noticed a question that asked for "specific likes and dislikes while hiking in the Adirondacks." Without thinking twice, I wrote down "being accosted to take surveys in the middle of my hike." I then handed back my form and motored down the trail.

Thank heavens I was not asked to conduct formal surveys while performing my duties, although I guess that might have been the most efficient method for obtaining all of the information that I was supposed to collect. I say this because the list of data was quite extensive. And by the end of our first ranger training week session, I was a bit mind boggled by all of the stuff that someone in the past had clearly decided just had to be put in a report someday.

We had forms. Lots of forms. To this day, I still honestly believe that they were all made up by a host of different administrators who did so without ever talking to each other, as many of them appeared to ask for the same information. It was almost humorous.

I actually became pretty good at polling our users for information without their knowledge, although this involved memorizing the forms so as not to forget some of the questions. Information such as hometown, number of people in the group, routes selected, and campsites used were diligently recorded for later tabulation at a Secret Tabulation Center that was probably located some- where under a mountain in the High Peaks. The information must have been classified as top secret as well, as I never saw the results of any of the reports we were required to file.

I felt truly sorry for some of my cohorts in the more heavily traveled regions, for they must have had to carry reams of the stuff with them. I wouldn't have had the patience. (Or the strength!) But then again, it was seldom that I ever met up with anyone in the West Canadas, and I often waited for two or three days at a time to record my findings. And sometimes even that was unnecessary, as I'd occasionally go for an entire week with- out meeting anyone.

Encountering total solitude for one whole work week brought its own set of challenges, as we also had a set of forms dedicated to justifying our time. As I recall, we were given choices such as "hours spent on public relations" and "hours spent on public edu- cation." (This can be pretty darned hard to do when there's no public to educate or relate to!) I avoided a possible hassle with this form by ignoring it altogether.

The forms that we were given asked for a plethora of infor- mation, which we were to then summarize on a separate series of "summary forms." This information, presumably, would show the average land use, including data such as the numbers of campers utilizing individual sites within our respective territo- ries. We were supposed to turn these figures in on a regular basis to someone in our regional office, who would then forward them to the Secret Tabulation Center (which may or may not have existed).

It rarely happened. No matter how hard I tried, I couldn't quite master the art of filling out all of the forms to the point where I (or anyone else) could make statistical sense of them. And even when I did, I often didn't get around to turning the papers back in to the people who distributed them in the first place. Not that I didn't try; I did. But somehow I just couldn't get it done.

At times, I even set defined deadlines for myself, which I swore that I'd adhere to. "I'll turn them in by the first of the month. I guarantee it," I promised them, even though I doubted that it would ever happen. And usually, it didn't. As a matter of fact, I'm sure that my superiors at the office must've thought that I was totally illiterate. Before too long, whenever I promised them anything by "guaranteeing" it, they looked at me doubtfully, as though they trusted my good intentions but didn't believe that I'd actually get it done.

One of my saving graces was the administrative staff at the DEC office in Northville, where I received my biweekly paychecks. Without their help, guidance, and understanding, I would have never received a cent. I cannot say how many times I was lectured to about the timecards that I was supposed to complete and submit "in a timely manner" to ensure that I was paid. And after all, if I couldn't be counted on to submit my own timecard, what could I be counted on for?

Not a lot, I guess, as it, too, never happened. Throughout my entire tenure as a wilderness ranger in the West Canada Lakes, I never submitted a single timecard. I was saved by one of the friendly secretaries, who must have taken pity on me (which was certainly easy to understand; she only saw me in one old and tattered set of clothing, and I was driving a vehicle that was held together by the rust spots.) For three years, she faithfully submitted my pay record, complete with a "substitute" signature, to ensure that I'd receive my stipend. I do hate paperwork.

But as bad as I was in the administrative functions of my position, I feel certain that I was not alone in my suffering. At the various get-togethers with the other wilderness rangers throughout the years, I'd heard stories about some "alternate uses" for the forms that filled our packs, one of which included a paper airplane distance throwing competition from the top of the Blue

Mountain fire tower. I, too, attempted various versions of origami when I manned the Pillsbury Mountain Fire Tower in 1979. By carefully folding the wings of the paper airplanes at different angles, I learned how to manufacture a model that would do several circular laps around the tower before finally reaching the ground.

As the first season progressed, I found that I was carrying fewer and fewer of these forms until I eventually left them behind entirely. Instead, I waited until I was out of the woods each week, at which time I used my general note pad, which I always carried, to stir my memory and complete the forms as best as possible. To this day I'm glad that I used this system, as that note pad contained many of the names and details of the people described in these chapters.

When I finally left the territory following the 1981 season, I decided to try to make up for some of my former administrative ineptness. I wanted to do so by providing the state with a valuable compilation of the resources of the entire West Canada Lakes and Silver Lakes Wilderness areas. It was a major piece of work, and I knew that it would require some amount of time to complete. But I was determined. And I had already promised the Regional Forester that I would deliver it within the first month after leaving the job.

For a few days, I labored intently over the project. Then, gradually, other concerns got in the way, and the resource survey got moved to the proverbial "back burner." And the only reason that I still remember this undertaking at all is that I found part of it a couple of years after leaving the job. It was packaged neatly in a box in the attic of my parents' house, waiting to be completed.

I removed it gently from its container and examined the beautiful leather cover that I'd purchased to hold the final copy. I turned the pages of the work that I'd started years earlier, noting the painstaking effort that I'd put into graphing (to scale) the campsites, lean-tos, fireplaces, and other resources of the territory that I'd patrolled. Not bad work! Not bad at all!

It was then that I decided to finally complete the volume and ship it off to the regional office in Northville. After all, the land and the facilities and the lean-tos were all still in their original locations. The study would certainly still be of use to someone in the DEC office, right? And this time, I promised myself, I would really get it done. "I'll turn it in by the first of the month," I said to myself earnestly. "I guarantee it!"

—7—

The Forest Primeval

The very remoteness of the territory, combined with the sparseness of hikers and campers, meant that we would encounter visitors on an infrequent basis. But during the middle of summer, when school was out of session and the majority of workers took their vacations, the woods could be full. This was especially true on weekends, when lean-to space was often at a premium. However, the weekdays were usually less crowded, and other factors such as rain and insects tended to diminish the population even further. John once remarked to me that "a few days of rain each week would be a good thing," as it discouraged some of the less serious trekkers.

For my part, it didn't make much of a difference. Unlike John, who always had a bit of hermit in him, I was a fairly social creature. Even though we were encouraged to remain somewhat distant from the hikers who passed through, I often shared a lean-to and a communal fire with these individuals, taking comfort in their friendship and the stories passed over the nightly flames.

However, it was during the rainy periods, when the skies opened up for days on end, that the woods really emptied out and a person could find solitude for longer periods of time. It was then that I started enjoying the quieter depths the woods had to offer, what I liked to call the forest primeval.

Before I spend too much time describing the wet weather that permeated the woods during these times, I'd like to say that it didn't have to be raining for one to experience this primitive state of the woods. There were several places that seemed to be quiet and dark regardless of the weather. Usually, these were in particularly remote locations, such as the bouldered stretches of West Canada Creek on the west side of Mud Lake or the off-trail outcroppings west of Cedar Lakes. There, the depths of the forest and the metamorphic rock formations made for a darkened woods that shielded the ground from the majority of sunlight. At places such as these, the dense tree canopy or the sometimes cave-like rock formations seemed to shut out the rest of the world regardless of the weather. But these areas were not part of my official patrol route, so I seldom visited or stayed long.

The phenomenon of the forest primeval conjures up images of an endless woods that is tall, dark, and forbidding. Quiet and deep and magical, it is seen by very few. It closes down around you and seals you off from the outside world.

This description hardly seems to fit even a territory as large and empty as the Adirondacks. After all, almost all of the park has been forested at least once in its lifetime, and signs of man's intrusion can be seen in most places. Yet, there were areas in the West Canada Lakes region where, on special days, the woods reverted to this primitive state.

The arrival of rain was almost a requirement for reaching this condition, as it rid the woods of a good many people. (It's difficult to feel very remote when you are surrounded by crowds.) Additionally, a bright sunlit day, with golden rays shining through the trees and warming the ground, did little to lend the woods a forbidding quality. The forest primeval experience usually required darkness, with clouds and a slow, cold rain that dripped through the trees and dampened the ground below.

The presence of large rock faces always enhanced this feeling for me, and I noticed it every time I passed by Cobble Hill at the end of Cedar Lakes. This protective jumble of giant boulders and rock formations once served as a temporary camp for Adirondack French Louis. It was he who discovered and slept in an almost perfectly square, roofed room formed by the ancient deposit of rock.

Passing this natural phenomenon on rain-soaked days was almost a mystical experience for me. The granite-grey rock seemed to close out the rest of the world, as the water dripped down its face and flowed into the soil. The skies grew darker and darker, and layers of thick clouds blocked out everything from above. It was as though the world was shutting down around me, cutting off my lifeline to everything outside the forest.

The smell of the conifers was thick in the air, as was the damp odor of rotting soil beneath my feet. At times there was another scent in the air, that of the invisible deer, nestled down in the leaves and thickets, quietly watching. I did not recognize that smell at the time, only wondered what it could be. It was not until years later, when I read French Louis' description of the "smell of wet blankets," that I realized its origin. There were other signs of deer in the area, but I did not stop to search. I only walked, step after quiet step, through the almost impenetrable darkness of the woods.

The side "feeder" trails to the Northville-Lake Placid Trail also presented some wonderful places to observe this deep woods phenomenon. One spot in particular was the Sampson Lake end of the trail between Sampson and Pillsbury Lakes. On the Pillsbury side of this trail, the route widened into a dirt road that was passable via all-terrain vehicles, thus removing any illusion of a deep forest. However, as you got closer to Sampson, there were some beautiful rock formations that cropped up on the south side of the trail. This was another place where the rain and the fog closed down all perceptions of space and time. As night descended on this spot, the coyotes could be heard howling in the distance, their lonesome songs adding to the feeling of utter desolation.

In a different era, this had been a busy stretch of woods, with trails branching off to Whitney Lake and southward towards Otter Lake and Balsam. However, that was years earlier, and even by the late 1970s, those trails had vanished into the forest, reclaimed, as always, by nature. I had spent some time searching for remnants of the Otter Lake trail, scanning the woods and walking search patterns for telltale reminders of these long-lost paths. At times, I felt that I had found stretches of trail marked by lengthy ruts in the ground or an old blaze on a tree. But I could never be sure, and I couldn't find a continuous route that didn't finally yield to unblemished swaths of birch and maple.

During several of these explorations, I became conscious of the spirits of woodsmen who had gone before me. Perhaps they were the original men who had cut those trails and were now laughing at my inability to follow their paths. I looked at the woods, trying to visualize them in their day and time, calling me to follow them into their forest primeval. But try as I might, I could not see them, any more than I could see their roads. Their laughter evaporated into the mists that swirled through the thickets beneath the darkened woods.

These solitary experiences made we wish that I was not assigned to a rigid daily patrol schedule that told me which trails to hike each day and where to sleep at night. These routes were designed by our boss, forest ranger Tom Eakin, to provide the maximum amount of coverage and exposure to the public as possible. Tom had put a lot of thought into these schedules, and there is no doubt that they did their job. As long as I had a partner (which I did for the first two years), we were able to cover almost every route and every lean-to each week. But still, those deeper woods called.

My only guilt-free incursions into the wilder places were on the occasional Wednesday and Thursday "weekends," when, for one reason or another, I decided to stay in the woods on my days off. This seldom happened, as I usually took advantage of those days. However, I enjoyed these interludes of unscheduled seclusion, as they allowed me to venture into places not often seen by human eyes.

On one of these trips, I forged a route southwest of South Lake towards Mica Lakes. Although only a distance of a couple of miles through fairly open woods, it still felt oddly primitive. Here, the forest was quiet, except for the call of the occasional sparrow or swallow. The terrain was a gently sloped pattern of rolling hills, punctuated with patches of rock and swamp. All traces of human existence disappeared within the first half mile of my trek, replaced by an ever-deepening sense of solitude.

The same was true when I ventured down the West Canada Creek, which flows out of Mud Lake and widens into the dark and meandering waterway that will eventually find its way westward, passing through a series of still waters in route to a crossing under Route 8 in the town of Ohio. I never made it very far down that route, which is dense and clogged with alder thickets. Within the first mile of leaving the Placid Trail (which crosses over the creek), I was immediately hit with an overwhelming sense of isolation. The woods around the creek appeared deeper, thicker, and more remote. They closed down around me, rendering the solitude an absoluteness that was almost palpable. There was no need to look for any footprints in this territory. I was alone, so very alone. If anyone was ever hurt in this area, they would be at the mercy of God and their survival skills.

As I picked my way slowly along, hoping to reach even the first stillwater, I was again greeted by the aura of the woodsmen from another day. Those men, who pioneered the woods over a hundred years before, would stop and wonder at my hesitation. They were trappers and hunters who thrived in the forest primeval. The deeper, the better. With little direction (and the absence of reliable maps), they found their way through the woods in all seasons and all kinds of weather, catching or shooting their meals as needed.

Within a half day of tumbling over rock-lined creek beds and climbing up and down over endless embankments, I decided to reverse my path and head back towards a more "civilized" woods. Certainly, my sense of curiosity had been met, and I had been privileged to travel to places that might not have been visited in many years.

Forest primeval? Perhaps, although those hunters and trappers of yesteryear would probably not agree. To them it was home, and it may never have been deep enough or quiet enough to satisfy their passion for absolute wilderness. Still, those woods are out there today, waiting, beckoning, and calling out for anyone who seeks the seclusion they have to offer. Quiet. Dark. Silent. And majestically alone.

—8—

Fire Tower Fraternity

When I applied for the job of wilderness park ranger in 1979, I had no idea about the adventures and experiences that lay ahead. Within a few short months, I was living a lifestyle that very few individuals born in this century would ever experience, and for that I was grateful.

I was also grateful to my boss, Tom Eakin, the forest ranger of Speculator and Lake Pleasant, for looking out for my continued employment. For as we reached the last weeks of August in 1979 and our ranger season rapidly approached its end, he offered me a chance to remain in the region through the end of November. Instead of being on the trails of the West Canada Lakes, I would be in the fire tower on top of Pillsbury Mountain, a 3,600 ft. peak on the southeast side of my original territory. It wasn't quite the same as walking the trails down below, but it was still a cabin in the woods with a view that included parts of Cedar and West Lakes. It was also eight miles from the nearest paved road, so I was assured of some degree of privacy.

New York State originally used fire towers as the sole means of spotting and reporting forest fires. Naturally, a fire tower can see only as far as its unobstructed range, which in the Adirondacks can be quite limited, so the state erected a series of 108 towers, which were spread throughout the Adirondacks, Catskills, and other forested locations that required an observant eye. It was an impressive array that required extensive staffing and continuous maintenance. Those were the days before fire flights began taking over these duties, eliminating the need for the towers.

In general, I found that fire tower observers fit into one of two categories. There were the old-timers, who had been up on their mountains since time began. (An exaggeration here, but not much of one if you consider the years some of the guys spent up there.) They were senior citizens who had lived up in their cabins and towers through thick and thin and had seen the passing of numerous storms, fires, and other natural cataclysms. In a few cases, they stayed up there on their days off because the weekly climbs up and down their respective mountains had grown too arduous for their legs. These were the men who had the best sense of their territories. Even as their eyesight was on the decline, they could detect the slightest change of hue on the horizon that might have indicated the birth of a wild blaze. I enjoyed these fellows' company immensely and tried to learn as much as I could from them.

The other category of observers were the younger folks, myself included, who were up there for the sole purpose of experiencing a truly unique and possibly vanishing job. (Try asking a group of your friends whether any of them have ever served as a fire tower observer and see how many "yes" answers you receive!) We ranged in age from mid-twenties though late thirties and had spent an average of two to five years on top of our towers, although many of us were in our first or second year

One of the things that I learned quickly was that, perched on top of my own private mountain with my own private radio tower, I could hear radio operators across the entire state talking to each other. This was a new and different experience for me, as I had grown accustomed to the limited reception down in the sunken valleys of the West Canadas. From down in those recesses, I could hear Pillsbury Mountain and my partner if he was standing within spitting distance. But that was about it. The chances of hearing anyone outside our own district were about zero.

Up on top of Pillsbury, the radio was constantly abuzz with radio transmissions from across the state. Many of those other voices belonged to the forest rangers and environmental conservation officers of our district as they went about their business, primarily law enforcement and compliance, which was of little interest to me. However, there was some occasional chatter between the observers, which always drew my attention. We weren't supposed to talk unless there was official business, and this "lack of radio discipline" was frowned upon. However, it did happen from time to time and was a welcome relief to my day.

Even when nothing else was breaking the silence, you'd hear the various observers signing on and off throughout the day, for lunch, trail work or other necessary projects. And the day ended with each observer signing off the air with the words:

"Pillsbury Mountain (or whatever mountain it was), station KH5279, will be clear and out of service at 1700."

It was a solemn procession of voices that signed off every day as the sun dipped low, and I listened intently to the observers on Wakely, Cathead, Blue, Kane, Gore, and Hadley mountains. Somehow, they represented a fraternity of brethren with whom I felt a connection. We were all in this together, each of us on our own perch, watching over the forests of New York.

Within my first week on Pillsbury, I decided that I wanted to visit some of those other voices. It's not like they were from another universe; many of them had towers that were within an hour of my own, plus the time required to climb down my mountain and up theirs.

Before I ever had a chance to get over to any other towers, I had a visit from Rick Miller, the observer from Kane Mountain. Rick is an interesting fellow who remains a good friend to this day. He had already been on top of Kane Mountain for several years when I met him and he was very knowledgeable about the towers and observers of the region. He filled me in on the locations of the various tower trails and the personalities of the observers. It was a useful and entertaining visit.

One of the few towers that I did not need to visit was Wakely Mountain. Wakely was situated just to the north of my ranger territory and was manned by another good friend, Peter Gloo. Pete was one of the new types of fire tower observers. He was quite young, energetic, and full of personality. He was also into trying to learn how to build mountain furniture, which was a pursuit that fascinated me as well.

The reason I did not feel a need to visit Pete was that his mountain was already old news. Throughout my months on the trail, we had conversed often on the radio, and I had ventured up his peak on several occasions. An avid outdoorsman, Pete had taken upon himself the task of restoring the top of Wakely Mountain to its original splendor. He was always fixing up something, removing years worth of accumulated trash, or building something new inside the cabin. Pete had a riveting personality, and I thoroughly enjoyed his company.

As Pete's interest in the woods grew, so did his love for furniture building. He became quite adept at constructing furniture out of small limbs of trees that grew near the top of his mountaintop lair. Although he constructed several pieces that were worthy of mention, there was one that was more impressive than all the others. It was a couch that was big enough to seat three people comfortably. It was about six feet long with sturdy legs and a lengthy series of smaller branches that appeared to be either cherry or yellow birch. I couldn't tell; the shiny red bark looked as thought it could have belonged to either species.

In any case, this particular bench was meticulously crafted.

Peter had gone so far as to carry finishing nails up to the cabin to make certain that the job was done correctly. The final touch, however, was never completed. Peter wanted to bring up a series of comfortable cushions, which would rest on top of the lattice of branches. Whether he was too busy or his pack was too full I will never know. But the pillows never made it to the top of Wakely Mountain, so the hard branches lay exposed for the sitter to sit on. This was unfortunate.

I never figured out a way to tell Peter this, but the couch was not comfortable. When asked to take a seat there, I complied, hoping that our session indoors would soon end. Within ten minutes, I could feel the knots of the branches biting cruelly into by back and seat. Within twenty minutes, I felt certain that the pattern that was impressed back there would become a permanent part of my anatomy. At that point I'd start coming up with reasons to get up.

"So, Pete, what do you say...let's go outside for a while and check out your front lawn! Looks like you've really put in some work out there!" I'd say.

"Sure, Larry," Peter would reply. "We'll go out later and take a look around. I'll be happy to give you a tour. But first, let's sit for a while and have a cup of tea while you tell me what you've been up to."

"Certainly," I'd counter, trying all the while to find an excuse to stand up. "I'll fill you in while we take a look at your tower. Wow, it sure does look good! Did you paint it this year?"

Back and forth we'd go, me trying to get us out the door while Pete seemed intent on staying inside. For the life of me, I couldn't figure out how Peter himself didn't seem to notice the lumps and bumps of his creation. In any case, I sometimes preemptively terminated our conversations by excusing myself to use his outhouse. Hey, any port in a storm, right?

Unfortunately, Peter only remained on top of Wakely for a single season, then he resigned to pursue a career in music. (He was a talented piano player who would command a good job and salary in any city in the country.) His departure created a double void; first, he was a friend who would be leaving and not returning to our area anytime soon. And second, the state decided that Wakely Mountain was not a critical tower, and the observer would not be replaced the following year. It was sad to see the tower from time to time after that, knowing that it was vacant and falling prey to those people who would vandalize the cabin for the sole sake of destroying property.

I also had a chance to visit some of the towers on the southern end of District Ten, including Kane and Cathead. Both of these were really glorified hills rather than mountains, which caused some troubles for the observers.

On Cathead, which was located north of the headquarters in Northville, Dave Slack had a cabin that was barely a ten minute stroll from his trailhead. While I envied the ease of his hike in, I was also thankful that my own cabin was so much less accessible. Dave had trouble whenever he left the woods, since anyone with a casual whim could break in and remove his possessions when the urge struck. I was on the opposite end of that spectrum, since my own cabin was eight miles into the woods via a dirt road, then another two miles and 1,600 feet in elevation removed from the world. I had very few visitors by comparison, and I rejoiced about that.

In fact, the tower on Cathead was so accessible that my first visit was during the pitch black of night. Rick Miller, who was also a friend of Dave's, talked me into coming along for a surprise visit one evening when we were down in Northville. While I was doubtful about climbing a strange trail in the dark of night, I quickly found that the trail had little in the way of steep climbing and also very little in the way of distance. It represented the perfect job for someone who wanted to serve as a fire tower observer but didn't want the exercise that went along with the job.

Another one of my early climbs was up Hadley Mountain,

where one of the old-timers named George had been in residence for many years. Hadley was also one of the lesser climbs in the area, although the trail did wind its way up over almost 1,000 feet in elevation. The tower was located near the boundary between Warren and Saratoga counties. I had heard that it offered some outstanding views in almost all directions, and I looked forward to seeing it.

Unfortunately, I wasn't a big news observer when I decided to climb Hadley. I was on duty and I hadn't paid attention to the weather reports or the national news. Had I tuned in that week I probably would have abandoned any thought of being outdoors and instead remained in my cabin.

The day I had selected to climb Hadley was Thursday, September 6, 1979. For those readers who are not meteorological fans, I should mention that this was the week that marked the end of Hurricane David. This storm, which had its origins in the balmy waters of the South Atlantic and Caribbean Sea, became a virtual monster as it tore across the southern United States and into the eastern part of the country. A Category 5 storm, it resulted in damages in the Caribbean alone totaling over one billion dollars. Property damage and loss of life were extensive from the Dominican Republic through much of the eastern seaboard and New England, with coastal damage in the United States exceeding one hundred million dollars.

I had little or no inkling of this as I climbed out of my car on that rainy Thursday afternoon. After all, hadn't I hiked through the downpours of the West Canada Lakes for the past five months? I was used to whatever Mother Nature could throw at me, and then some. A little bit of rain certainly wouldn't cause me undue harm, I thought, as I pulled on my heavy slicker and pack cover. I was certainly ready for the elements. In any case, I knew that George, the observer, would be waiting up top in his cabin and would surely let me in to dry off. In fact, the rain could even make for a better visit, as he wouldn't have to mind the tower in the rain. We could just hang out in his cabin and trade tower stories for the afternoon.

As I fastened my slicker around me, I laughed at the fact that I usually chose to forego this garment. In light-to-moderate precipitation, I found that I could get wetter from my own sweat than from the rain. However, today was an exception. The rain was coming in a steady downpour and made a loud splattering sound as it ricocheted off the hood that was covering my head.

As I started up the trail that afternoon, I noticed that I was walking through significant pools of standing water. The trees overhead may have shielded me from some of the direct rainfall, but the water coming off the trees seemed to be of equal flow. To quote a line from the famous Doctor Seuss, "It was a wet wet wet day!"

As I slogged onward, I kept expecting the rain to abate somewhat. Instead, it intensified. The raindrops got bigger and harder as the wind velocity increased. I had never hiked in such conditions and was having a hard time getting into my standard mindset of ignoring the elements. This was extreme.

By the time I made it to the steeper part of the climb, where the rocky outcroppings served as steps for a hiker, I discovered a new phenomenon—whitewater on the trail! It was not a stream, but a raging torrent that pushed its way down the path in a tumble of cascading waterfalls, doing its best to prevent me from reaching the top and enjoying my day off.

The rest of the climb was more of the same, only perhaps worse. The rain never let up, and the wind played havoc with my progress. Even standing upright was a task at times, as I leaned forward to counter the strength of the elements. Hurricane David was no longer a genuine hurricane at this point, but it certainly was a mighty storm. It was a stupid thing to do, going climbing during the peak of this downpour. But hindsight is always 20-20, so there I was.

By the time I arrived on top of the mountain, I was completely drenched. I could not have been wetter had I jumped into a lake fully clothed. The water on the trail had been pouring downhill and into the tops of my boots, so even those were saturated. I had every expectation that had I removed them at that point, I would have discovered a small fish or two inside. I was wet.

As I squished my way over to the observer's cabin, I counted down the number of steps it would take me to climb the stairs and walk inside. I really wanted to get dried off at least somewhat and have something hot to drink. I had never met George, but I knew he'd welcome me inside and help me out of the storm.

Then, I saw it—the closed door with the note tacked to the outside. I didn't know what it said, but I knew that it wasn't good news. This cabin had the look of a locked, unoccupied building. As I climbed under the front door overhang, my eyes tried to will some print onto the note, something that would read, "I'm inside—please come in for a nice hot cup of coffee!"

Instead, the sign provided the standard note used by most observers when they were off the mountain. "I'm out doing trail work. Please leave me a note or return later." Yeah, uh huh. I knew with certainty that George was not in the woods, having probably left before the storm started. There would be no relief from the rain for me until I walked myself out of the woods.

There is no point in continuing my description of this wet and miserable day. It remains as the worst weather in which I have ever hiked. I can only blame myself for not checking on the conditions before leaving, and I should be thankful that my return trip to my car was uneventful and safe.

Later on that summer, I did have a chance to meet George. But this time I waited until the forecast was good and I knew that he would be in residence on top. I brought him a package of blueberry muffins as a present to break the ice, as I found that many of the old-timers were somewhat more reserved than my contemporaries.

George took me up into his tower and showed me the 360

degree view, which was quite impressive. We spoke at length, and he told me of his dealings with Smitty, who was the old-timer who had manned my Pillsbury tower for many years prior to my arrival in the area. George had worked up on Hadley for a long time, and he was very comfortable with his surroundings.

The only thorn in George's side appeared to be the telephone extension which was strung up to his tower. This was something that I did not have on Pillsbury. My phone went only to my cabin, and even this was non-operational for most of the fall. But George's phone was very functional, although I think George would have preferred otherwise. During our visit he received a number of calls, all of which appeared to upset him. To this day, I'm not sure whether they were from his wife or from another source, but he did not appear to be pleased when the phone rang.

After a short time, I took my leave and headed back down the mountain. I was not sure whether George had appreciated my visit, although I hoped that he had. His quiet nature and reserved personality had restricted our conversation to matters of fire towers and other work-related topics. I felt as though he was happy to meet me, but it would require a lot of time to develop anything in the way of friendship.

Gore Mountain, on the other hand, was a totally different matter. It was manned by another old-timer who happened to share my first name, and he was a character from the word "go." I had given Larry some advanced warning that I'd be paying him a visit, so he was prepared for my appearance. Then again, I think he was prepared at all times for anyone to show up, since his fire tower was built on top of a mountain that was also a popular state ski facility.

I had looked forward to meeting Larry from the first time I heard him on the radio. He had a slow, base voice that just boomed over the speakers in my tower and a distinctive and deliberate drawl that carried a hint of some time spent in the South, although I don't believe that was the case.

I had formed a mental picture of a big man with a weather-creased face who could handle any and all emergencies with a single swing of his axe, so I was surprised when I met Larry, because he was actually a very small, thin man. The only thing that was big about him was the pair of dark green sunglasses that he wore, almost dwarfing the rest of his face. As I emerged from the woods and ascended his tower, he gave me a handshake and a smile that just illuminated the place. It was quite a contrast to my welcome on Hadley, even though it was simply due to his effusive personality.

Larry signed off, and then led me down to his cabin for some lunch. It was not like any other cabin I'd ever seen. The entire area was covered with roads for the ski facility, so almost anything you might want could be hauled up there without undue effort. Most tower cabins were small log affairs with a very rustic appearance, but this one had the look of a small house like you'd see in the city. It was pretty much standard in dimensions, although it had some luxuries that most of us did not have, such as electricity.

I took a seat inside the cabin and listened to Larry weave stories about his years on the mountaintop. He was a real character and well known among the local population. As he spoke, he cut off round lengths of hamburger from a meat log and began to fry them in a cast iron pan.

Over the next hour, he showed me pictures from an album that displayed some of the history of the mountain and the facilities, including the tower. He was another one of the experts who could tell you the exact location of a fire based upon the color and direction of the smoke. As a matter of fact, he had the dubious distinction of once having to call the fire department to extinguish a blaze in his own house down in the town, which he spotted from atop the mountain's tower! I heard this story from a third-hand source, but he supposedly lost everything he owned in the blaze and had to start over again with just his insurance money.

After visiting for a couple of hours, I said farewell and headed back down the mountain. I was glad to have met Larry, for I would now be able to put a face with that glorious voice I'd heard signing off every day. He and others like him were the true faces and personalities that colored the history of the Adirondacks, and I was pleased to get to know a few of them while I still could.

Each time I climbed another tower that fall, I tried to spend as much time with the observer as possible. Sometimes that was difficult, as some of them were very busy with the flow of visitors that passed through their tower. Such was the case when I stopped up to visit Gil Goodnough, the observer on top of Blue Mountain. Blue is located near Blue Mountain Lake, close enough to the Adirondack Museum so that it draws major crowds. I only climbed Blue Mountain twice that year, and both times I found Gil surrounded by visitors.

"You wouldn't believe it," he confided in me during a quiet moment in the tower. "I can get several hundred people up here in a single day, if it's a weekend and the weather's nice. I don't have time to take care of my basic needs. It's crazy! I don't know why they don't hire a separate tour guide and just let me do my job."

When I told him that my log book on Pillsbury showed an average of about two hundred visitors for an entire season, he was incredulous.

"I can get that in a day...or easily in a weekend. You don't know what you've got over there. You want to trade mountains?"

"No, Gil, sorry, but no deal," I laughed. "I'm not cut out for this kind of duty. I'd probably end up in jail for pushing someone out of the tower. I just couldn't handle it."

Gil was upset and appeared to be just getting started. "You don't have any idea how it is up here. I can't even take a lunch break most days because people want me to let them into the tower. Heck, I'm not going to leave them in my tower by themselves.

Lord knows what I'd find when I got back. They'd probably try to make off with my map table. And my cabin, you can forget about that, too. Sometimes I come down and try locking the doors while I eat a quiet lunch. Nope—no way. Someone is always knocking on the door to ask directions, or to get a picture of me doing something outside. I think I've about had it with this place!"

I commiserated with Gil for a good part of the afternoon, as we stayed up in the tower and traded stories of our time in the woods. It turned out that Gil had heard many of my radio transmissions while I was down on the trails that summer with my portable radio. I had heard him transmitting from Blue on one or two occasions, but that was possible only from a few select locations. As we watched the non-stop flow of hikers come up over the top of his mountain and start climbing the tower stairs, we amused ourselves with stories of the more inexperienced or inept visitors. Wisely, we waited for breaks in the traffic in the tower to exchange these anecdotes, but I was amused to find that Gil had even more funny stories than did I. He was an interesting man with a great sense of humor, and I enjoyed his company.

Within the span of a month, I had climbed just about every active fire tower in our territory, along with several of those that were vacant. Some of these, including the tallest one, located on Snowy, had been empty for years and were in very bad need of repairs. In most cases, the state had already decided to abandon these towers in favor of the fire flights, much to the dismay of the old-timers who worked the peaks back in their heyday. The public also wanted to save the towers and replace the observers on top, but their complaints fell on deaf ears. The funding was running out, and the fire flights represented a cheaper way of monitoring the fire status of the great north woods.

My last day as a fire observer was just a few days before Thanksgiving. I knew that I'd be back in the woods next year, serving in my primary duty as a wilderness park ranger. As I shut down the tower and prepared to lock up the cabin, I wondered whether I would be the last observer ever to serve up here.

This wonderful location, which some said was the most remote of all of the 108 original fire towers, had been my workplace and my home for the past several months. During that time, I'd had the pleasure to climb many of the other towers and meet most of the observers. We were all part of that very small fraternity of individuals who worked in these extreme settings, high above the cities and towns, in some cases without human contact. At the end of the day, when the sun went down, we were left to ourselves, each of us a single person on a mountaintop with a view of the world.

As I prepared to disconnect the radio from the batteries, I felt a bit wistful. This last act would separate me permanently from those voices which had become my friends. But it was time to sign off and head out of the woods. Part of me was tempted to say a brief farewell to my friends, although I quickly decided otherwise. Better to keep it short and professional in order to maintain strict radio discipline.

I kneeled down on the floor of the cabin, ready to pull the wires that would save the batteries for a future observer. Then, with my head bowed, I pressed the transmit button and sounded my final report.

"Pillsbury Mountain, station KH5279, will be clear and out of service in thirty seconds at 1700."

Olympic Experiences—Part I

To say that John Giedraitis greatly affected my life in the late 1970s would be a vast understatement. It was John who, while a roommate and fellow student at the SUNY College of Environmental Science and Forestry in 1978, first convinced me to apply for the wilderness park ranger program.

John was an outgoing and very likeable fellow, and his enthusiasm was contagious. Several of his suggestions, made casually over a late-night glass of beer, were responsible for adventures or other aspects of my life. He had a way of talking about people and places that made you want to experience them yourself.

So it was no wonder that John's phone call to me during the winter of 1979 got me thinking about the Olympics. I had recently come out of the woods as the fire tower observer from Pillsbury Mountain. This job, which had been arranged by my boss Tom Eakin (forest ranger of Speculator/Lake Pleasant), had allowed me to remain in the woods through the end of November. This was great, because most of the wilderness park ranger jobs wrapped up shortly after Labor Day.

After leaving the woods, I stayed with Patty for a week or two and then returned home to New Jersey to be with my parents. I seldom saw them during the summer months, although they did drive up to Speculator on occasion to visit.

John's call came in during the middle part of December, and he was excited. I could hear the anticipation in his voice.

"How would you like to go up to Placid to see the Olympics with me?" he began, whetting my appetite for the experience. "I have a couple of contacts up there who can get us jobs right on the bobsled and luge tracks. We'll be there, front and center, in the middle of all the action. It'll be like seeing the Olympics from inside a television set!"

I didn't ask for too many details, as I knew that John probably didn't have many answers anyway, you know, to "small" questions such as where will we live? Things like that were never a problem for John. They were mere triflings, to be worried about at a later date and time. For now, the main thing was just to get up there.

As I said, John was a good talker, and he quickly convinced me to join him in his latest escapade. And why not? I really wasn't doing anything besides killing time at home, and the pay was a pretty decent hourly wage with rumors of significant overtime. I was ready!

By the time I met John in Lake Placid, I was feeling a bit less confident about our adventure. To begin with, I had never been able to accumulate a great deal of cash, and right now I was a bit lighter than usual. I needed to start working as soon as possible, as my last paycheck had been consumed by gas and other bills. We had no place to live, and we had yet to even fill out job applications for our Olympic work. Perhaps this wasn't as good an idea as it originally seemed.

One of our biggest hurdles was that the houses in Lake Placid were all renting at prices that were well above our means. And those prices were still at pre-Olympic levels. Heaven help us once the price-gouging started and the average three bedroom place would go for three thousand dollars per week. We didn't know where we would stay.

Getting a job was a little bit easier. John used his contacts to get us in the door at Mount Van Hoevenberg, where the Olympic bobsled and luge tracks snaked side-by-side down the mountainous terrain. True, they weren't glorious jobs, but they were paying jobs. We were assigned to work as laborers on the outdoor runs, maintaining the tracks and preparing them for the Olympic competitions. It would be cold, rigorous work, but at least we would have that "up close and personal" view of the Olympics that we so desired.

John and I pooled our money to secure a place to stay. Unfortunately, even between the two of us, we couldn't come close to the asking price of a cheap apartment. This left us in a real bind, and we spent our first few weeks on the job scrambling for places to lay our sleeping bags at night. Not that we needed much in the way of comfort, as we had both spent part of the past few years sleeping on lean-to floors or at primitive tent sites.

For a few nights, John was able to get us into the hiker's building at Heart Lake, where we sacked out after they locked up at night. However, we soon wore out our welcome and were forced into the back of John's station wagon. Not a very comfortable arrangement, considering that there were two of us plus John's dog, Kazak.

By the time we received our first paycheck, we were both ready for some genuine accommodations, something with real beds, a kitchen, and a shower. Unfortunately, we discovered that the rental prices throughout the entire area were high, not just those in the direct neighborhood of the Olympic venues. But after much searching, we were able to locate a house in Saranac Lake (about ten miles from Lake Placid) that seemed to be within our size and price range. We quickly called the real estate agent listed in the advertisement to arrange a meeting. It didn't have to be fancy, just functional.

The house was neither fancy nor functional. Our first clue about this was the fact that it had no front door. Someone had either stolen it or removed it and never brought it back. The open doorway beckoned us forebodingly into a dark stairwell which led to the second floor apartment.

"This place has been empty for a while," said the agent as she struggled with an ancient key lock at the top of the stairs. "I can't guarantee that it's in good shape, but at least it's a place to stay at a reasonable price."

As she opened the front door, we had our first look inside. Whoever last rented the apartment had obviously left in a hurry. The place was a mess. Food had been left out in packages for an undetermined length of time, and dirty dishes filled the sink. The kitchen and living room were littered with papers, garbage, and other unrecognizable bits of trash that had been left there by the previous occupants. The bedrooms, both small and dingy, were similarly filthy, with the additional mess of dirty clothing that had been thrown about. The place was an absolute and insurmountable mess.

The woman from the rental agency turned towards us and gave us an apologetic grin. Then, speaking in an encouraging voice, she made a proposal that we couldn't refuse.

"Well, it's a bit worse than I thought," she said, "but nothing that a few trash bags can't handle. And I'll tell you what. I was going to charge you $250 a month, but how about I'll knock it down to $175 if you'll take care of the clean-up?"

Feeling as though we had some wiggle room given the mess, I tried adding in a quick bargain.

"Wow," I said, looking around with a scowl. "This is going to take us several days to clean. Plus, we'll have to buy curtains for the windows, since the last renters must have removed them when they left. So how about this: we'll give you the $175 a month, you'll let us slide on the security deposit. We're both state employees and very reliable. We're also new on the job and very low in cash, so I'm afraid that it's either that or nothing."

She appeared to be satisfied with the deal, and we shook hands on the financial arrangement. Then, she left, leaving us to the arduous task of cleaning out the heaps of garbage.

The two of us decided who would have which bedroom. Then, we split up and started on opposite ends of the place. Armed with an entire box of large garbage bags, we started shoving the nameless odds and ends into the bags and carrying them downstairs. We both wanted to make sure that we had cleaned out our respective bedrooms by nighttime of the first day, and even that was a challenge. It didn't take long before the entire front of the house was lined with trash bags for the weekly pick-up.

As it turned out, my prediction (about several days of work) proved to be true. It was about three days later when we "met in the middle," peeling the last of the junk off the floor and walls in the living room. We'd soon have it ready to host friends, but for now it just felt good to be able to see the carpet and furniture throughout the place. Even the kitchen was cleaned sufficiently to appear both neat and inviting. So, for a very reasonable price, we had obtained an acceptable place to sleep.

The job on the mountain, however, was a bit of a different story. It was all about ice: how to make it, shape it, and replace it. I learned more about ice that winter than I thought possible.

If you've never seen a bobsled or luge run, you're in for a unique experience. Picture, if you will, a massive garden hose that is six to twelve feet in diameter that winds its way down the side of a hill. This hose takes numerous turns, often approaching 360 degrees, and then reverses course in a series of violent zigzag patterns. Now, cut that hose in half lengthwise, so that only the bottom of the hose exists, resting in the snow along the mountain. Voila, you have a luge run!

The bobsled and luge runs have more similarities than they do differences, and the unfamiliar visitor might confuse the two. However, the bobsled run is actually much bigger, both in size as well as in length. It is roughly a mile long and can have walls that approach twenty feet in height. The luge run, on the other hand, is both shorter and smaller, with many similar curves and straight-aways as its bigger brother. Additionally, it has two different starting gates, one for women and another one (higher up the mountain) for men. Approximately one third of the vertical drop of the entire course is found between the men's and women's starts.

By the way, the sport of luge is basically designed for grown-up children who never got over the thrill of racing their Flexible-Flier sleds downhill in a dash to the finish line. Modern day luge sleds, while not really resembling those sleds of old, share a great many features with them, including a pair of polished metal runners and a flat deck on which the slider (or luger) reclines while riding downhill. Steering is accomplished by moving the feet and shoulders on the sled and by creative use of other body movements. It is a fast and exciting sport, but still one that awakens our desire to return to the big hill of our youth for that one last ride.

John and I were both assigned to the luge crew, whose job it was to maintain the ice on the track in perfect condition at all times. This is a difficult task, especially when you consider the fact that you've got about one thousand yards of ice, all of which is being subjected to the constant stress of the luge sleds passing over it at speeds exceeding sixty miles per hour.

We learned the very first day on the job that working on the luge crew was a tough assignment. The crew members were all local boys who prided themselves on their rugged, sometimes outwardly combative natures. It was not the kind of place where you talked about your college major. Far from the scholarly athletic types who filled out the ranks of the wilderness ranger corps, these men were all blue collar workers who had spent their lives laboring for an hourly wage. They frequented a particular bar in Lake Placid on weekends because of the "great fistfights that break out from time to time." Pain was not an issue. Toughness and the ability to fight were the highest-honored traits.

Despite their show of aggressive behavior, I found that many of these folks could be approached on a friendly basis, especially if they determined that you were a good worker. As a result, I spent my first few weeks shoveling and scraping ice like there was no tomorrow. I wanted to make a good impression on my new coworkers, and work ethic (in lieu of being a good fighter) appeared to be the best solution.

Usually, we started at the top of the track and moved down it in unison, with some people shoveling, some people sweeping, and still others patching any holes that they might find. There were about a dozen of us on the crew, and most of these folks were pretty good workers. I found that by conserving some strength until the final fifty feet of track, I could put on a really good show, shoveling snow up into the air and out of the track, and reloading before the last batch even hit the ground. At times, it resembled a snowblower, and I always attracted the attention of my fellow crew team members.

The foreman of our crew was a short, fiery fellow named Tuffy. I never did find out his real name. With scraggly hair and a very full beard, he looked perfectly in his element while standing outside in the Adirondack winter air. Tuffy could be very friendly or a raging madman, depending on the situation. I quickly decided to try and remain on his good side. By always giving my best physical effort (including the snow blower routine), I was able to do so.

I knew I'd won Tuffy's confidence one day after about two weeks on the job. I was being introduced to Foster, the man who managed the night crew, when Tuffy came by. Slapping me on my shoulder, he said to his counterpart, "This is my bull! I call him that because of the way he works around here. And no, you can't have him! He's on my crew."

The days on Mt. Van Hoevenberg followed each other in a blind fury as we prepared the track for the Olympics. From morning until night, sled followed sled down the mountain, and we followed the sleds to ensure that the ice held up. In some places, we had to create slush from ice and water to use for patching holes. In other spots, we needed to use a tortuous tool called a roller chisel to remove excess ice that caused the sleds to jump. This tool was a five-pound, metal chisel that had small wheels inside the casing. The person wielding this device had to keep sliding the chisel head up and down along the icy curve, adding enough pressure so that the blade removed the offending ice build-up. It gave the user an extreme physical work-out and could probably have served as its own Olympic conditioning device.

To say that conditions up on the mountain were severe could be an understatement. During the day, the sun kept things at a manageable temperature, although it sometimes struggled to get much above zero. However, at night, the mercury sank to incredible lows, sometimes reaching twenty to thirty below zero. There were many occasions when, having shoveled and swept and pushed our way to building up a good sweat, we would find ourselves covered with ice by the time we reached the bottom of the trail. Beards and mustaches froze solid, giving us a truly bizarre appearance. On some of these days, we worked so hard that we had to remove our coats, regardless of the outside air temperature. Imagine the stares from the visitors as they watched us toiling away in shirtsleeves, despite the below-freezing temperatures. On days like that, the steam literally poured off of our bodies like the exhaust from a sauna bath. It was quite a sight, and we ourselves became part of the spectacle of the track that was so frequently photographed.

These working conditions, when coupled with the exposure and the cold air, produced some truly magnificent, hacking coughs, and nobody was immune to these. We had a break room at the top of the mountain where we would stop for coffee, and it often took on the sounds of an old-fashioned TB ward. Coughing and hacking and wheezing, we would shuffle in and remove several layers of winter clothing before grabbing our hot beverage of choice. It was not a pretty scene, although very few people ever called in sick. Perhaps they couldn't afford the loss of pay, because the attendance rate remained quite high throughout the entire winter. Part of me is still willing to believe that this might have also been due to the whole image thing: "I'm tough enough to stay out here and work while I'm sick, and so should you!"

Before I give the impression that we were all work and no play, I should admit that there was a fair amount of "shovel sliding" that got tossed into the work day. What is shovel sliding? Simple! Just grab anything that will slide down the track at a rapid rate of speed and climb on board! This included a plethora of slippery objects, some of which were designed for the purpose, while others were not.

One of the most commonly used devices for sliding was the standard snow shovel (thus the name). The shovels that made the best sliding platforms were those that were not overly wide, with flat bottoms and angled side wings. This allowed the rider to sit in the shovel, holding the handle pointing forward between the legs. If the rider desired to stop, he or she only had to pull up on the handle, and the edge of the shovel would dig into the ice. Leaving the handle alone would allow the rider to accelerate, especially on the upper part of the track where the slope was the greatest.

I had to admit that I was quite leery of these makeshift sliding platforms and the recklessness with which my co-workers rode them. To be injured while going fast or doing something acrobatic was considered to be a great feat, while refusing to ride was an act of cowardice. The office that managed the tracks, which sat at the bottom of the mountain, deemed this form of entertainment to be against the rules. However, they had a very hard time enforcing this policy, as these workers were not overly impressed with adherence to regulations. "Sliders" from our crew regularly flew past the open window of the office, even when they knew that they were being observed. With the Olympics coming on within the next month, there was not a lot the bosses could do, as the area had very few experienced luge and bobsled track experts waiting in the wings to replace those who might be fired. So the sliding was unofficially tolerated.

Having no desire to lose any of my fingers, toes, or other critical body parts, I waited until a fellow worker (who was not known as a daredevil) offered me a ride on the back of his green plastic sled. After all, I reasoned, this wasn't a shovel, or something else that could injure me. This device was made for sliding and should offer some form of protection, right?

I knew within ten seconds that the ride was a mistake. Starting out from curve three above the men's start, Steve's sled rapidly accelerated to a speed that made my eyes pop. As we passed the on ramp for the women's start, I felt my eyes glazing over with tears, which then proceeded to freeze my eyelids to my cheeks. I couldn't see, I couldn't breathe, and on top of everything, the world was rushing by at a truly astonishing rate. I would have been OK had I managed to keep my left hand inside the sled for the entire ride.

However, someplace right outside the giant Omega curve, we hit a bump that sent my left arm flying out of its protective cradle for just a second. That was all it took as we flew past one of the wooden guards on the lower portion of the course. And that is where I left my finger, permanently affixed to that stretch of track. Or so it seemed at the time.

By the time we arrived at the final out ramp, we had slowed to a very controlled pace. Steve got out first, followed breathlessly by yours truly. I was really hoping that my ride had convinced the other crew members of my fearless nature and reckless intent. However, nobody was in sight, so it was all for naught. I would have to find another way to impress them.

I was certain that my finger was broken in many places, and

it indeed felt quite painful to the touch. However, after some careful and tender ministering, I was able to bend it and rotate it through most of its natural positions, thus avoiding a trip to the emergency room (and incurring the scorn of the crew).

Later that week, following an unusually easy workday, we all decided to end the day with a serious sliding session. With a twinge of excitement, I announced my intention to solo from the top of the men's start. Additionally, I would ride one of the faster shovels in the inventory and would try to accomplish the entire ride without braking.

I have always felt that I am a fairly sensible person, although I do sometimes get caught up in the moment and part with some of my ability to reason. In this case, I must have parted with all of it. I don't know what was going through my mind when I volunteered to go on this suicide mission, but I was already in too deep to back out. The rest of my cronies gathered round as I started my slide from way above the rest of the mountain.

Performing a pretty fair imitation of the lugers who rode this hill during the day, I used the starting handles to rock back and forth, thus giving myself added momentum for the big push down the hill. Then, with a final heave, I let go.

The first twenty feet of the ride weren't bad, until I realized just how steep that first hill was. By the time I hit the straight-away to curve one, I was flying along at over thirty miles per hour and accelerating by the second.

In order to accurately describe what happened to me and my body, I need to give a brief description of the fine points of luging. The luge track has both curves and straight-aways. When a straight section of track is about to enter a curve, there is a rounded corner of the track known as the "take-on" (or that's what we used to call it), which allows the luger to enter the curve gracefully. By entering the curve on the take-on, he or she will stay low and thus preserve the optimum path through the curve. However, if the luger misses the take-on, the main wall of the curve will be hit head on, throwing the luger violently up the wall and into a series of uncontrolled gyrations. There is a real possibility of injuring yourself, so this should be avoided whenever possible.

I didn't know about any of this as I sped down the icy path, cheered on by the hollering voices in back of me. By the time I reached the gentle bend of curve one, I was going over forty miles per hour. (One of the trainers occasionally put a speed gun on us, so we had a fairly accurate idea of our velocity.) With a little bit of skill and a lot of luck, I cleared curve one in fine fashion.

Then, all hell broke loose.

Up ahead was the giant, looming form of curve two. It was a wicked, ninety degree curve to the right, followed by a very short crossover into an equally huge third curve, which bent back to the left. As my body hurtled towards the curve, I tried in vain to remember just what I should do in order to survive the rapid whipping that I knew I'd experience flying between these two extreme turns. It was sometime during this action (or lack thereof) that I flew past the take-on to curve two without ever seeing it.

I hesitate to even venture a guess as to the frightful speed I had attained as I became airborne while going up the great height of curve two. All I knew was that I wasn't supposed to be up there and that I was going way too fast to do anything about it. I was at the mercy of two natural laws of the universe— gravity and acceleration. And neither of these laws were working in my favor.

From the top of curve two, my shovel scraped along the bare wood of the structure. This caused a rapid alteration of my path through the curve, and I was thrown downward in a sickening plunge to the ice at the bottom of the curve. I was still moving forward at an extreme rate of speed, and I thought that I just might have a chance of making the crossover into curve three. However, that was not to be. Instead, I flew sideways (still riding the shovel) and crashed into the solid concrete wall inside the barrel turn. I hit with such impact that the hardwood handle of the shovel disintegrated in my hands, with splinters being thrown far and wide inside the track and out. I skidded for another sixty to seventy feet, finally coming to rest at the bottom of curve three.

I'm not really sure what I felt at that point, or if I felt anything at all. My entire right side was numb from the impact, and my mind was in a daze. As I lay there on the ice, I could vaguely make out the sounds of the others running and sliding down the ice, following (albeit more slowly) to find out my fate. Good question. I was a bit uncertain about that myself.

By the time they caught up to me, I had pulled myself into a sitting position. With some degree of amusement, I noticed that the top eighteen-inch section of the shovel handle was still tightly gripped in my fist. Where the metal part had come to rest was anyone's guess.

"Wow, that was great!" shouted someone, patting me on the back with enthusiasm.

"Did you see that crash, man? That was awesome! You're a madman, guy!"

Others followed with similar remarks, while the rest of the crew just stared at me with wide-eyed expressions of disbelief and admiration. All the while, a little voice in my head kept saying, "I don't believe I just did that. I've got to be the biggest fool in the world! Never, ever again will I be talked into pulling such a stupid move!"

However, I couldn't voice that sentiment to this group of new admirers. Despite my professional background and my college education, I was now OK in their minds. I had performed my initiation feat and was now a member of their club.

—10—

Olympic Experiences—Part II

The winter of 1979-1980 was a memorable time for Lake Placid, which was enjoying the buildup to the start of the Olympic Winter Games. The same town had hosted the 1932 games as well, although there were very few individuals who still remembered those competitions.

For us, hard at work on the luge and bobsled tracks, it was a chance to get everything just right. While our responsibility was limited to a thin, one thousand yard long strip of ice, we wanted to make sure that it was in perfect shape for the start of the games. We shoveled and shaved and glazed that ice until it was perfect, with not a hole or bump in sight.

On the day that the athletes arrived, we stood by at attention as they did their customary walk-through. Starting at the very bottom of the track, they slowly walked the entire length of the run until they arrived at the top. They studied every curve, line, and straight-away on the course. Quietly, they discussed their thoughts and strategies with their coaches and teammates. In most cases, I couldn't hear their conversations, and I wouldn't have been able to understand them even if I had. Each team brought a new language, and there were many nations represented. As each one paced the track, I began to wonder just how all of these athletes would have time to slide in the same competition.

That first day also brought an array of color and pageantry. Each team was adorned in its own uniform colors, with coordinating spandex outfits, shoes, warm-ups, overcoats, and head gear. It was all very impressive when they marched past, forming an unofficial parade up the hill.

In a way, we were part of this uniform parade as well. To improve our appearance for the Olympics, the Lake Placid Olympic Committee had purchased complete outfits for all people working on the mountain. Some were fancier than others, and you could tell where people "ranked" based upon their garb. For us, they provided a very nice set of insulated denim coveralls decked out with the Olympic logo of those particular games. A yellow turtleneck shirt, woven of an early insulated synthetic material, was our primary undergarment, and a woven wool cap (again with the official logo) completed the outfit. Additionally, each member of the track crew was given a pair of insulated, rubber "Mickey Mouse" boots. These boots were truly amazing and could keep your feet toasty warm in the most frigid conditions, even when standing in six inches of frozen slush.

Because this was my first Olympics, I was unaware of the customs and traditions that accompany the games, and I was puzzled when the first coach passed me on the track and handed me a pin. It was an ornate one, showing a stylized luger whizzing past a red, rising sun. It was from the coach of the Japanese team, and it carried a few Japanese symbols or letters on the bottom, also in red.

I looked at it dumbly as it sat in the palm of my hand, trying to figure out why the coach had given this to me. I looked up at him as he looked back at me, somewhat questioningly. To avoid complete embarrassment, I smiled and nodded my head in acknowledgement. He returned my smile and bowed back to me.

He also spoke some words which, whether in Japanese or in English (I couldn't be sure), I could not understand. And then he was gone.

Whether I knew it or not, I had evidently passed my first course in international relations. At least I hadn't accidentally insulted anyone. And now I was prepared for those teams and coaches who followed one after another on their scouting walks. The pattern was the same—every coach who passed by presented each of us with a pin. I wondered whether that was a gift for preparing the track so well, or a tip for future favors that we should provide. No matter. I stashed my growing collection in my front pocket and continued with my work. I eventually accumulated enough of the memorabilia to fill an entire beer mug.

The start of the actual Olympic Games ushered in a lot of other changes in the area surrounding Lake Placid. For one thing, the flow of automobile traffic was highly restricted, and special passes were required to drive inside a certain radius of the town. A road block was established on Route 73 to the east and at some predetermined location in each of the other directions as well. Beyond those points, it was either show your pass or turn around.

Inside the town of Lake Placid, other changes were occurring, many of which I felt were detrimental to the spirit of the games. Restaurants raised their prices dramatically, and several of them were rumored to have placed a time limit on the length of a meal. This angered a great many people, and hordes of them avoided the eating establishments entirely. It was interesting to note that a lot of the wealthy-looking spectators on the mountain were walking along holding takeout bags from the Grand Union grocery store. This confirmed my opinion that rich people don't mind paying premium prices, but also that they don't like being "had." By the end of the games, both the time limits and the increased prices had disappeared, although not in time to salvage the profits that some of these merchants had desired.

In the real estate market, the simplest apartments were

going for ridiculous prices. Our own agent tried to double our rent, to which we had to cry foul. We knew that we were too far away from the games to attract other bidders to our house and that the general rundown appearance of the place did not lend itself to most of the winter tourists. Still, we knew that she wanted more money, and that she would try her hardest to get it.

What we hadn't counted on was that she would show up at our door, ready to come in and discuss the matter in person. This was a problem, because she had specifically told us prior to moving in that there were no pets allowed, and John had then proceeded to move in Kazak, his black-and-white spaniel-mix dog.

By the time I opened the door and saw her standing there, it was too late to do much about that. I only prayed that John could grab Kazak by the collar and corral him in his bedroom before the landlady saw him. It was close, but he made it, collapsing in a silent heap on his bed. He pulled Kazak up onto the bed beside him and held him by the muzzle, willing him to keep quiet.

The landlady stood in the doorway looking into the kitchen. "Is your roommate here?" she asked in a polite but expectant voice. "Because I need to talk to the both of you about the rent for this apartment. It's going up next month for the Olympic Games, and we need to come to an agreement as soon as possible."

"Oh, no, John's not here," I lied, feeling the hot flush of blood on my cheeks. "He's out at a friend's house, although I expect him back in time for dinner. Just how much do you plan on raising our rent?"

She didn't answer me. I looked at her, standing silently in front of our stove, her eyes fixed on a single object. I followed her stare and cursed myself when I saw their target. There, sitting on the floor in front of John's bedroom, was Kazak's dogfood bowl!

In a quiet, stifled voice, she asked me "Just what is that? You know there are no animals allowed in this house!"

I didn't know what to do. The entry to John's room did not have a door. All that prevented anyone from seeing into his room was a simple woven tapestry, which had been attached to the top of the door frame with a series of evenly-spaced thumb tacks. If John or Kazak had so much as breathed, both of us in the kitchen would have heard. I took a deep breath and prayed that my luck would continue.

"Oh that! Yes, I'm sorry. I really am. We had a cat that wandered in here earlier this week. He came up the stairs all by himself and entered while we were bringing in groceries. I probably shouldn't have done this, but I gave him some leftover chicken from last night's dinner. I do apologize, really I do."

She looked at me narrowly, trying to figure out whether I was sincere or not. "Are you sure? Will you promise me that you have no cats living in here with you? Because if you do, I'll find out. I swear I will!"

With that, I turned to her and gave her my most sincere expression. "I promise you, on my honor, we have no cats living with us, nor will we ever have a cat living here." I've never been very good at telling people things that weren't true. However, in this case, I had no problem at all, since (I reasoned) I was being completely factual. And since she never asked about the origin of Kazak's bowl, I let the topic slide.

From there the conversation shifted to the pending increase in rent, which would have been very tough for us to afford. I decided to appeal to her compassionate side, if she had one. After all, nobody really wants to be responsible for making some-one homeless, and this is what I implied.

"Oh, that's OK," I began my plea. "I know that you can't help it. But we can't afford the new rent, either. How about this? Could we sleep in the stairwell for a few weeks, just until the rent comes back down? Please? It would be cold, but at least we won't get snowed on at night, and the hallway light bulbs might provide a little bit of heat."

"You want to what?" she asked incredulously. "Sleep in the hallway? Why would you want to do that? Just give me an extra hundred dollars a month and you can stay here!"

"Oh, that would be impossible," I countered, "unless we could do without eating some meals. Yeah, I guess we could do that, although we usually can't afford three meals a day now. Sometimes we only have dinner and perhaps a glass of milk for breakfast. But don't worry; we'll get by somehow. Now, when did you need that extra money?"

Before long, the extra rent had been reduced from double, to $200, and finally back to our original sum of $175 a month. All the while, I was praying that my lengthy deliberations didn't result in a bark, whine, or loud whimper from Kazak, who must have been wondering why John had such a tight grip on him. It was extraordinary!

With a performance that was worthy of an Academy Award nomination, I told our landlady about a few ways that I knew to make five dollars last for a week of food, including the recipe for my famous rice gruel. (This was a box of rice, a small amount of hamburger meat, and one can each of corn, peas, and beans stirred together into a huge pot, then seasoned with salt and pepper. I had actually started cooking this during my poorer days as a graduate student in Syracuse.) She listened with simulated interest to the recipe before beating a hasty retreat out of the house.

As soon as she left, John and Kazak emerged from the bedroom, with John grinning from ear to ear while Kazak sang a song in a high-pitched whine.

"I thought we were toast there for a minute," said John. "You were great! How did you come up with all that stuff so quickly?"

"I had to," I replied. "What else could I do? If I screwed up, we'd be kicked out of here for sure, and we'd never find another place this close to the Olympics. It was do or die time for all of us. And by the way, *great job* keeping Kazak quiet!"

We celebrated our good fortune that night by having a beer toast at the Waterhole in downtown Saranac Lake. We had won the battle and escaped the rent hikes that so many others were experiencing at that time. It was a terrible practice that preyed on tenants who could least afford it, many of whom were displaced from their living quarters because of these disreputable tactics.

Around the physical area of Mt. Van Hoevenberg were more reminders that times had changed. Being a wilderness ranger, I thought that I was pretty observant of my surroundings, able to pick up the slightest sounds and movement from the woods. Over the past year I had noticed my increased ability to detect even the smallest of noises around me. From the fluttering of a bird's wing on a branch to the distant rising of a trout to the water's surface on a quiet day, I thought I heard them all.

Then, one day, from out of nowhere, we received the surprise of our lives. We were taking a shortcut up the side of a hill, walking behind one of the track's many curves. As we cut across a snowy expanse of open land, we were suddenly surrounded! A group of military men, completely dressed in white cold-weather gear right down to their boots, appeared out of nowhere, outnumbering us many times over. They were fully outfitted with radio gear and automatic weapons, ready to spring into action at the least sign of trouble. We stood there, frozen to our spots, as we eyed their weapons with trepidation. They, on the other hand, seemed little bothered by us; they were in the middle of an exercise that happened to cross our path at an unexpected moment. We said nothing, and then continued our trek up the hill. They in turn quietly retreated to the edge of the woods, melting quickly into invisibility.

I later learned that these were special Army troops which had been deployed to handle any potential terrorist threats. I was glad to learn that they were there if needed, but I could have used a bit more warning prior to their appearance.

Ah, well, if all these preparations and contingencies were really necessary for the Olympics to proceed, then so be it. Personally, I could have done without the back-to-back scares from the landlady and the Army SWAT team, but that was life.

We headed back to the top of the mountain and found the rest of our work crew, which was getting ready to commence another top-to-bottom sweep of the track. It was time to get back to work. Maybe I'd even find myself another pin.

—11—

Olympic Experiences—Part III

Being an employee at the Olympics was a great experience for a number of reasons. Besides being able to participate directly in their success, we also got to benefit from some of the many perks that came with working on the facilities. One of these benefits was that we could attend any of the events that were not sold out. These leftover tickets were available for free to employees, and we gladly took advantage whenever possible.

The event that we chose to see most often was hockey. Although not a fan of the sport myself, I did elect to attend a number of games that did not involve either the United States or Canadian teams, since those were the ones that were always sold out. Interest in ice hockey was very high that year because of the U.S. team, especially once they started to enjoy success against some of their stronger opponents (a precursor to the wonderful events that followed later).

The Olympics of 1980 had its usual share of heroes and heroines, as well as those athletes whose names will be remembered for lesser reasons. But the name that shined above all others during those games was that of the American speed skating champion

Eric Heiden. Heiden was making an unprecedented bid to win five gold medals at various distances, and he was making good on his promise. With perfect form and legs of steel, Heiden consistently left his competitors in the dust as he sprinted around the track, lap after lap. It seemed only a matter of time before he won the final event and claimed his spot in history.

I had decided that I, for one, wanted to be there when he completed his historic sweep. I knew that it was something that I'd never have the chance to see again, and I didn't want to be left out. Even though the tickets were extremely expensive, and I did not have a lot in the bank, I purchased a pair of tickets to see Heiden skate in the 10,000-meter finals, figuring that I'd treat John to a seat at the same event. I was surprised that there were any left when I got to the front of the line, but finally I had them! I also took the opportunity to purchase two tickets for us to see the Sweden versus Romania hockey game, which promised to be a great match.

Because of our busy schedules, we didn't have time to attend many of the daytime events. We often worked from sunup until sundown and then struggled home with aching muscles just in time to crawl into bed and recuperate for the next day. However, we did track Heiden's successes and were pleased to see that he continued to win medal after medal, each one gold, until he arrived at last at his final competition, the 10,000-meter race. Although Heiden had some tough competition that day, most of the skating world felt that it would be his race to win or lose, and most Americans thought he'd be up to the task, skating in front of his home fans. It would be a meet to remember for posterity.

John and I arranged to leave work early that day in time to get to the speed skating track early. The track is located right on Main Street on the lower part of town, within a short walk of the ice skating arena. We drove back to Saranac Lake to take care of some house-related matters and ate a small meal while there. John knew that he was staying late in Lake Placid that evening, so he decided to drive his own car. Not a problem. That way we could meet up at the track and take separate cars back home.

As we were leaving, we reminded each other to bring our tickets to the event, thus avoiding a catastrophic mistake. I shuddered to myself at the thought of purchasing these valuable tickets only to forget them for the big meet. Yikes! I slid my ticket into my pocket, checking carefully (twice!) that it was still there. Ah yes, all set for some history on ice.

Driving into Placid was very difficult, even with our special passes. Often, we had to park a mile away from our destination, and this night was no exception. As a matter of fact, I had to park even further away than expected, and I found myself trotting at a decent pace to insure that I got to my seat in time to see the best competitors skate their rounds.

By the time I made it to the track, the event had already started, but that was not a problem. They skated in inverse order to their times, so the slowest skaters with the least chances of winning skated early, while the real medal contenders skated last. I would have plenty of time to see the really good distance skaters make their run, followed by Heiden's attempt at gold medal number five. John was already inside the track, probably watching the preliminary rounds leading up to the final pair.

As I approached the admissions gate, I reached into my pocket and extracted my ticket. I sure was glad that I had remembered to put it in a safe location! I tried to look through the fence to see either the track or John in the stands. Instead, the thick green canvas material lining the fence blocked almost everything from view. Absentmindedly, I handed my ticket to the guard who was admitting the spectators.

I tried pushing my way through the turnstiles to get into the track. Instead, I was met by a hand that blocked my progress. It belonged to the guard who had taken my ticket. Looking at me and then back at the ticket, he shook his head and spoke slowly and deliberately.

"I'm sorry, Sir, but you can't use that ticket to get into this event."

"What?" I screamed, flying into an instant uproar. "That's a good ticket that I just purchased from the official Olympic ticket issuer. What the hell do you mean 'I can't use this ticket....?'"

The gentleman looked back at me in sorrow, trying to explain himself before I had the chance to get even hotter.

"Oh, your ticket is valid, and you can use it. Just not to this event. You've just given me a ticket to see Sweden play Romania in men's hockey!"

In a second, I saw the folly of my actions. Not that I could do anything about it, but I felt as though I would get sick on the spot. I tried to reason with the guard, knowing that it would be of little use.

"But, but...but I did buy a ticket to this event. I swear, I did. As a matter of fact, I bought two, one for me and one for my roommate. I can prove it to you. Please, let's go inside and find him. I guarantee that you'll find an open seat next to him. That's my seat. Mine! I paid for it! Please!"

However, as much as the guard wanted to help me, his hands were tied. He had to remain at the counter to collect tickets, and anyway, we would have had a tough time spotting John amongst the thousands of onlookers. It seemed like a lost cause.

I looked at my watch and tried to calculate the amount of time that it would take to sprint back to my car, drive back to Saranac Lake, and then return with the correct ticket. By my approximation, if all went well, I might be able to make it in time to see the janitors and custodians emptying the trash at the end of the meet.

I hung my head in defeat and stood outside the fence, listening to the roar of the crowd as each successive pair raced faster and faster around the track. Then, long before Heiden's final match, I started the slow and depressing walk back to my car. I couldn't stand to stay there, listening to the sounds of Olympic history being made. I hoped John was enjoying the extra-wide spot on the bench seat. Of course he enjoyed the outcome, as Heiden destroyed the old world record by more than six seconds.

While this was perhaps my lowest point of the entire winter in Lake Placid, there were a lot of things that went very well to make up for it. Several times each week, they conducted awards ceremonies on the ice-covered Mirror Lake in the middle of town. With thousands of people in attendance, these gatherings took on a truly festive tone and gave us a chance to mingle with a lot of the folks who drove in solely to see the Olympics. We had a great time between the awards and the cheering and the food and drink, not to mention the toboggan run which propelled us down the steep, manmade hill and across the frozen lake. It was hardly an experience to match the high speed luge runs, but we all had fun.

We were enjoying ourselves to the hilt, with each night more celebratory than the one before. After all, we had to enjoy ourselves now, right? For soon, the entire world knew that we Americans would receive the trouncing of our lives when our men's hockey team faced the all-powerful Red Army team of the Soviet Union. Day of reckoning: end of fun and frolic. This would be the day that the music would stop.

Magic is a funny and very special thing. It never happens unless you believe. And on that cold, cold night in 1980, despite the doubts and opinions of the world, one very special group of young hockey players believed. And they weren't alone. As a single mass, the entire population of Lake Placid, men and women, young and old, doubters and believers, all came together to watch one special game. It symbolized so much to us that we felt we could will our team on to victory, despite the incredible odds.

Obtaining a free ticket to this game, or even purchasing one from a scalper, was downright impossible. The entire area around the arena was mobbed, including all of the bars and eating establishments. All television sets were tuned in, and all those watching responded as one whenever a Soviet or U.S. goal was scored.

We started believing that victory was possible when the U.S. made it to the third period, down by a single goal. Throughout the games leading up to this match, the U.S. team had owned the third period, due to it superior endurance and conditioning. We hoped and prayed that this game would follow the same script.

In the third period, the Americans pulled even and then took the lead with about ten minutes to go. By this time, we were all screaming at the top of our lungs. It would be the tensest ten minutes of our lives. Then it was six minutes. Then four, then two. And then, miraculously, the game ended with the United States still on top. Our college boys had defeated the Soviet professionals who had played together as a unit for over a decade.

The bar where we watched the game erupted into an immediate volcano of screams and cheers, with patrons jumping up on chairs and dancing on tables, and we were joined by the bartenders and the establishment owners. It was pure, unrestrained joy that knew no bounds.

Within the next ten minutes, the crowds spilled into the streets and merged with the patrons of the next bar or restaurant, and the one after that, and the one after that. Car horns honked, music blared, and every possible noise-making device was pressed into service. Main Street itself was elbow-to-elbow people, with everyone hugging everyone else and screaming in amazement. Even the few police officers I observed were getting into the spirit.

The party lasted long into the night and was still going as strong at one o'clock in the morning as it had been when the game ended. I would be lying if I claimed to remember what time we left the mass celebration. However, it didn't matter. Rather than risk driving back to Saranac Lake (since we had been guilty of partaking in the free flow of beer along with everyone else), we decided to sleep in John's station wagon that night and return in the morning. It was a night like no other, and I will remember it for the rest of my life.

The Olympics were also memorable because of the parties and gatherings sponsored by various corporate interests, television and radio stations, and national "hospitality huts." We tried to attend as many of these functions as possible, although we (as "common laborers") were never actually invited to the VIP events. But often, when a ceremony or reception was open to the public, we tried to find our way through the crowds and join the party. It was all part of the Olympic experience.

On our own mountain, things were a little bit more restrictive. As a group, we had planned to have a bobsled and luge track crew party, which would have been great. We were all looking forward to this event and had appointed several of our more responsible members to plan the function. Since these were all heavy drinking, blue-collar workers (whom some would call by the less politically correct title of "rednecks"), the party organizers had to insure that a sufficient quantity of beer was on hand to alleviate the thirst of the partygoers.

Not a problem! The plans for the party moved ahead rapidly until we were about a week away from the actual date. That's when we hit the snag. It came one morning when our foreman was down in the facility office at the bottom of the mountain and happened to mention our plans to one of the office secretaries. Word of an event such as that spreads quickly and soon made it to the ear of one of the top bosses.

"No, you're not," said the chief administrator of the facility. "You are not having a party with alcohol on this hill. Sorry, but those are the rules, and the decision is final!"

Well, that left us with two choices. We could either have a beerless party on the mountain, or we could take our celebration somewhere else. We conducted a quick survey of the two track crews and arrived at a unanimous decision. We would find another place to have the party. This conclusion was arrived at with little or no animosity towards the upper level management. After all, if those were the rules, those were the rules. We could live with that, although we would rather have held our party on our own turf.

Our sympathetic understanding of management's decision lasted for about forty-eight hours. That was the point when someone on our crew discovered management's intention to host a full-blown affair, complete with alcoholic beverages, at the bottom of the mountain. With a little bit of covert investigation, we were able to find part of their stash. Kirin beer, a Japanese import, was the official imported beer of the 1980 Olympics. In a corner of a large tent which had been erected below the luge track sat a pallet with ten cases of the stuff, ready to go.

To this day, I'm not certain what bothered the guys on the crew more: the fact that the managers had blocked us from having a party, or that they had ignored the rules when it pertained to themselves and arranged for an exclusive gathering, to be held one night that week after the site had cleared for the day. Regardless, the natives got pretty riled up, and we could detect that something nasty was in the works.

I'm not sure if anyone in our crew knew the exact date and time of the management party, but a few of them decided to swing immediately into pre-emptive strike mode. If they could have a party, we could have a party. And this party, it turned out, would be fueled by their pile of Kirin beer.

Much of what immediately followed was thought up on the spot by crew members who were too mad to worry about the consequences of being caught. They waited until quite late in the day, when the luging had ceased and the crowds had dissipated. This could occur quite rapidly, and the mountain which had been thriving with lugers and spectators could transform itself into a ghost town within an hour. At night, the only activity was the presence of the few members of the night crew, and that was it.

By about six o'clock on the evening in question, we were still at work, patching ice holes and getting the track ready for the next day. We detected no suspicious activities, although I did see two of our workers hop into the large utility truck and start heading down the steeply sloping road. This road was often covered with slick ice and snow, which the huge truck wheels managed to conquer much more easily than those of a passenger car. It was a huge old rig with a grinding transmission and a noisy exhaust system. In summary, it looked like it was on its last legs. And although it had a maximum speed that would probably never top thirty miles per hour, it sure could cover ground over snow!

Unbeknownst to John and me, the two crew members in the truck were on a round-trip mission to steal the beer from the reception tent. The plan was to bring the brew back up the hill and distribute it for an impromptu early evening party, compliments of the management! I'm not sure how many of my coworkers were aware of this plan, but nobody was discussing it as we started wrapping up work for the day.

The two crew members who made the beer run, Steve and Jeff, did everything according to plan. They made it down the hill as unobtrusively as possible and parked next to the reception tent. Then, in order to prevent detection, they slithered under the tent wall that was shielded from view from the office building. Having gained access, they proceeded to pass the beer cases in a two-man version of the old firemen's bucket brigade.

The plan was simple and straightforward. And it almost worked. If not for an alert staff member who noticed the truck parked next to the tent, Steve and Jeff could have completed their heist in peace and quiet. Unfortunately, this office worker was one of the folks who was involved in planning *their* party and knew exactly what to look for. Although the truck was already pulling out as he made his way over to the tent, he was definitely not fooled. And his next action was something that was not expected. He called the nearest police officials, who responded with lights flashing and sirens wailing.

Steve and Jeff didn't wait around for the posse to arrive. As a matter of fact, they felt very little in the way of sympathy when they noticed that the police cars were having a tough time negotiating the steep and slippery access road. They just pointed the old rig up the mountain and stepped on the gas.

By now, it was obvious to all of us on top of the luge run what was happening, and we quickly tried to figure out how to hide the crime. Here we were, cruelly exposed, with no place to run and the evidence of our theft arriving via special delivery, compliments of Steve and Jeff in the clunker truck.

What should we do? Most of us did not know that the theft had been planned, so we could claim innocence by non-participation. However, that would be hanging our fellow crew members out to dry, and we quickly decided not to do that. About four of the guys started unloading the beer as quickly as possible, while the police cars tried their best to climb the mountain. Their progress was slow, but we knew that is was only a matter of time before they arrived at our station. Things were looking grim.

As we stood there looking at each other, an amazing thing happened. We had a collective thought which seemed to dawn on everyone simultaneously. Here we were, about a dozen of us, standing at the top of a mountain with ten cases of Kirin beer. We had to make this evidence disappear as quickly as possible. And sitting there right next to us, just as pretty as you please, was a luge track with one thousand yards of downhill ice, just lying there waiting.

Yup, that's what we did! With each worker grabbing one case of beer, we rapid-fire dumped the contents of each case into the track, taking care to slide the bottles out without breaking them on the ice. To this day, I will never forget the sound made by ten cases of beer bottles, merrily sounding their "tink tink, tink tink" as they accelerated downhill and out of sight.

By the time the police were able to make it to the top of the mountain, we were in the break room below the top building, putting our tools away. One of the managers was with the officers, and there was clearly some hell to pay for the failed beer theft. However, there was little that they could do, since there was no beer to be found in the top shelter and no way to determine who had been driving the truck. (And, in the words of our foreman, "Ain't nobody seen nothin'!")

Needless to say, the beer was quickly recovered by the managers, although this time it was locked securely inside the office building. The eventual fallout from the whole thing was a further clampdown on our activities on the mountain, and all after-hours activities were strictly forbidden.

Later on that evening, John and I drove silently back to our house in Saranac Lake and filed up the stairs into our apartment. It was dark and cold inside, and we huddled next to the stove in the kitchen.

"You know, I didn't like the way we got roped into that whole thing today," John said. "We had no idea that our guys were stealing that beer, and yet we could have been arrested for it."

"Yeah, I know," I replied, knowing full well that our only saving grace (as a group) was that they couldn't arrest us all in the middle of the Olympics, as they'd have no one to run the track. "Incidents like that don't exactly make us out to be outstanding citizens. If there is anything I *don't* need it is an arrest record to follow me around forever!"

John agreed wholeheartedly, and then started to gently chuckle.

"You know," he said, "I can't help but laugh whenever I think of the sound those beer bottles made as they slid down the track. That tinkling was a dead giveaway. I wouldn't be surprised if the police heard the noise as they motored their way up the hill. It was actually pretty loud."

"Of course it was," I said. "Any time you knock together 238 bottles of beer, it's going to make some noise."

"What do you mean, 238 bottles?" John asked. He wore a perplexed look as he intently studied the expression on my face. "There were ten cases of beer, times 24 bottles per case. That makes 240."

"Ah, yes," I replied. "Your math adds up alright. However, you failed to take into account the complimentary beverage service that is available on all domestic flights!" Having said that, I reached into the front pockets of my oversized coat and withdrew the only two surviving bottles from the Great Beer Heist of Mount Van Hoevenberg. I set one before each of us and then reached for the bottle opener. "Drink up...the beer's on me!"

All in all, it had been a very good day.

—12—

Olympic Experiences—Part IV

Before anyone gets the idea that our entire crew throughout the Olympics was a bunch of low-life degenerates, perhaps I should take a moment to explain. Our people were all hard working, decent men who for the most part had families and children out in town. Most had some level of high school education, although none had ever attended college. They were avid believers in the work hard, play hard school, and that play could often get quite rough.

Another common bond among several of these men was that they had spent time in Vietnam. One of these veterans, a mainstay of the crew, was named Mike, and he was about as disciplined a person as I had ever met. Mike was not one to get into trouble, holding himself to the highest of personal standards. I also noticed an unusual trait about Mike that took me some time to digest. He never, ever took a seat unless it was against a wall. Mike liked being able to see everyone in the room, without having anyone sitting behind him. He wanted everything out in plain site. I felt that this had something to do with his need to control his own space, but I never asked him about it.

I later learned that Mike had completed two tours in Vietnam and had been badly injured during a fierce mid-war skirmish. He very seldom mentioned anything about the war, but he did relate to me the briefest of details one morning before our crew began work.

"I was running across a field near a rice paddy, trying to reach a couple of the other guys in my squad. All of a sudden I was thrown to the ground. I didn't know what had happened; I didn't even know I'd been hit. It turned out that I'd been shot through both legs and couldn't move. I was lucky that they found a way to evacuate me. I lot of my buddies back there weren't as fortunate."

I had always noticed that Mike appeared to be a bit bow-legged and that he walked with an unusual gait. This was accentuated as he pushed his way up the frozen surface of the track. But I never realized the reason for that peculiarity, which lay in his battle wounds.

There were others in the crew as well who had been educated in the school of hard knocks. They were good people who would give you the shirt off their backs, although they seldom had much more than that to their name. All of them supported themselves year-round on the hourly wage, which did not make for a cushy lifestyle.

These folks were also people who wanted to know where your loyalties lay and that you could be counted on when the chips were down. To some degree, I'd say that they were slow to accept you into their club, but would back you up with whatever they had once they did.

Their "work hard, play hard" attitude included some stunts that I thought were too strange to consider. Yes, I had survived a horrible, high speed, shovel-sliding crash going down the men's luge track. But these daredevils pulled off some feats which seemed suicidal to me. On one occasion, two of them rode a wheelbarrow down from the start of the Olympic bobsled track. They made it partway down before the barrow tipped over, throwing them out onto the ice. One sustained a concussion, while the other merely received a bloody gash on his forehead. But they both returned to the start house laughing about their experience.

Other instances of insanity were seen throughout the games. One of the night foremen had manufactured a special shovel with polished runners on the bottom, as though a regular shovel didn't go fast enough. However, the winner of the "I'm Crazier Than You" contest went to a fellow who, according to track crew legend, rode his bicycle down and off the seventy meter ski jump. Personally, I put that one into the urban legend category, although some of the old timers swore that it had happened.

Of course, not everything that winter was memorable. Between our broken-down tenement of a house and our aged (and often broken-down) cars, we had to make do on many occasions. There were a number of mornings when it was just too cold and our cars refused to start. I became very adept at the use of my right thumb as I hitchhiked my way to work on the mountain. (I often thought that people in my situation should be able to purchase special thumb warmers, to protect them during all those exposed hours along the frigid roadside.) Even purchasing groceries could be a major hassle when you didn't have reliable transportation and the sidewalks were covered with snow.

But, for the most part, it was a fun way to spend the winter. I learned how to use all of the various shovels and chisels and chippers and other tools that were required to maintain the track, and I probably got myself into better condition while doing so. Our evenings were spent either watching the competitions or engaged in friendly foosball matches at the Waterhole in Saranac Lake, a popular gathering place that remains in existence to this day.

Once the games began, the atmosphere on the mountain changed a bit, with the tensions of the competition reflected on the faces of the athletes and coaches. But for the most part, we remained on a friendly basis with everyone. We already knew all of the American lugers from their months of practice prior to the games. Once the Olympics commenced, we also came to know the Canadian and British competitors because they spoke our language.

Even those athletes from the European countries who spoke only German, French, Italian, or other languages came to recognize us, and (for the most part) appreciated our efforts. They showed this by rewarding us with a friendly pat on the back or presenting us with an occasional pin. (None of the crew members collected these, but they could be traded for one or more beers out in town!)

In turn, we tried to please everyone, although that was not always possible. I remember one particular afternoon once the games had begun when Mount Van Hoevenberg was obscured from vision by a sudden and furious snow squall. One of the German sliders (either East or West German; I can't remember) was in the process of making his run downhill. Their coach, with whom I had developed a friendly nodding relationship, stood nearby. His face was deeply creased by an angry scowl as he looked down at the snow that had accumulated on the track. This snow would slow his luger's progress, especially on the flat straight-aways where the snow could pile up the fastest. It would also make it very difficult for the person steering the sled to see, as it was whisked and swirled into an impenetrable fog-like cloud by the mountain wind.

I tried using my best sign language to point out that this was snow that had just fallen within the last two minutes and that there was *nothing* we could do about it. After all, once a squall set up, there was no way that a dozen men could rapidly clear two-thirds of a mile of ice track. It just couldn't be done. However, the coach overlooked my attempts at reconciliation and continued to glare unhappily at the snow. Needless to say, I did not receive a pin from him that afternoon.

Towards the end of the games, John and I hosted a party at our house, to which we invited all of the Olympic competitors from the United States, Canada, and Great Britain. None of the athletes showed up, but some of their support people did, and they explained that the lugers had a full schedule. Our neighbor in the front apartment decided to throw a party on the same night, so we put our heads (and our apartments) together and merged the festivities. For me, it was somewhat of a final shindig for the games. Cindy (our neighbor) knew a lot of the people who worked in and around the ice arena, and they all joined us for the evening. Our apartment (and even our bedrooms!) were filled with a slew of people, many of whom I had never met. But it was a great way to wrap up our stay.

As the games wound down, so did our activities on the mountain. The medals for the luge and the bobsled were awarded, and sliding was done. Even the practice runs had ceased on the luge track, although individuals could still pay to take a ride down the bobsled track from some midway point. This was always a popular attraction despite the hefty fee, for it allowed people to participate (on a safe basis) in a genuine winter Olympic event. From what I'd heard, tourists could even pay to ride in the middle of summer, when the refrigerated track was completely devoid of ice. Evidently, they attached special wheels to the sleds, allowing them to roll at a decent speed down the hill and across the finish line.

The track crew continued to operate after the games were done, since they still needed to maintain the track, albeit to a lower set of standards. However, I had already given my notice that I would be leaving at the end of the month. I had some plans in mind to visit Patty in Glens Falls and then to head south to see my parents in New Jersey. This would take me right up to the start of the ranger season in April.

My last day of work was somewhat anticlimactic. Much of the hard labor that we were used to was no longer necessary, and the weather was turning warmer. We weren't in as much of a hurry to get out onto the track, since nobody was sliding out there anyway.

I took a longer than usual lunch hour, sitting around the chipped plywood table in our break room. I also used this time to say goodbye to my friends, the other members of the track crew. As expected, we all promised to keep in touch, although I knew that our paths would never cross again.

Having bid my farewells, I strolled leisurely down the hill and punched out my timecard in the main office. With the first flies of the season starting to drone in the air, I climbed into my car and listened happily as it started on the first attempt.

I pulled out of the Olympic complex and turned south, pointing my car toward Patty, but also in the direction of the green mountains and clear waterways of the West Canada Lakes Wilderness area. They were beckoning to me to return, and I was eager to answer their call.

—13—

Down for the Count

I'm lucky that I was born with a good immune system. Considering all the abuse I've put my body through over the years, I've been blessed in experiencing very few illnesses. I have literally gone decades without missing a single day of work and can seem to remain healthy even when those around me are hacking and wheezing in close proximity.

Why this is so is a mystery to me, as I've never taken unusually good care of myself. I get much less sleep than my peers, I don't take vitamins (although I do eat a well-balanced diet), and I don't wear outer garments in anything but the coldest weather. Given all of these factors, plus the wear on my body from walking miles on the trails day after day, I'm amazed that I didn't spend at least a fraction of my time recovering in sick bay somewhere. However, that never seemed to happen, and I compiled a perfect attendance record for my three years as a wilderness park ranger.

All of this might seem irrelevant, as we weren't penalized for being sick. But with me, it was a matter of pride. I never wanted to call in with an excuse for not being on the job. It's just not my

style. However, one Friday morning as I arose to start my preparations for entering the woods, I had some serious doubts about
my previously unbroken streak of vigor. It wasn't even something
that I could define—just a run-down feeling, lack of appetite,
and general lack of energy. I didn't feel good.

As I prepared for the two-hour drive from Glens Falls to Perkins
Clearing, I had to push myself to complete even the simplest of
tasks. Eating breakfast seemed like a chore, and lifting my backpack into the trunk of my rusting 1971 Oldsmobile required a
Herculean effort. I felt myself perspiring needlessly as I slid
behind the wheel.

It was still relatively early when I hit the road in to Sled
Harbor, although the logging trucks were already going full tilt.[3]
It was August already, and I was in pretty good shape. However,
even on the flat parts of the logging road, I felt myself breathing
harder than normal. I usually felt better than this even while
ascending the steeper inclines of Blue Ridge. Something was definitely wrong.

The next half hour was a true indicator that I wasn't entirely
well. It was only a mile from Sled Harbor to the point where the
trail peeled off to the left to ascend Pillsbury Mountain. This
mile wasn't all that difficult; it was mostly uphill, but at a fairly
easy grade over a wide dirt road. This was nothing that ever tired
me in the least, and I could motor along at a fairly rapid pace up
this stretch.

But not today. As I moved along up that hill, I felt as though
each of my boots had been filled with lead. My breath was
labored, and I felt the sweat trickling down my back. And on top
of everything, something inside me just felt wrong.

I made it up to the trailhead for Pillsbury Mountain and then
stopped for a short break. I had never stopped there in the past,

[3] Today, the public can drive a car past Perkins Clearing and right up to the trailhead for Pillsbury
Mountain, although a four-wheel drive vehicle is needed for the last mile beyond Sled Harbor.
However, before the land swap between New York State and International Paper, a gate blocked all
public vehicles from going beyond Perkins Clearing. This added three miles on to my hike each week.

but I felt as though I needed the rest and the drink. As I stood there in the cool morning shade, I seemed to hallucinate, thinking that I heard an engine coming at me. It was a motor, perhaps of a small all-terrain vehicle, but definitely a motor. It sounded pretty distant, the droning barely detectable to my ears. It was going through cycles, first louder, then quieter, piercing the morning quiet.

As I stood there contemplating this phenomenon, the noise became louder and more recognizable as a genuine engine. It sounded like a good-sized vehicle, and it was moving up the ridge in my direction. In my slightly delusional mindset, I wondered who it could be, since the only person who had a key to the gate (Tom Eakin) was down in Northville that day. I never stopped to think that it was illegal for anyone else to be up there in a motorized vehicle. Instead, I just stood there in a trance, waiting for this thing, whatever it was, to arrive.

I didn't have to wait long. Within a minute, a pickup truck crested the slight rise before me and coasted to a stop. From the driver's seat I saw Larry Lawrence's smiling face beaming out at me. Larry was a local from Speculator who owned and operated one of the popular eating and drinking establishments in town. He also owned a camp that was situated down the Pillsbury Lake road, which is now referred to as the French Louis trail. He was an extremely nice person who was well liked and respected in the area, and I always enjoyed talking with him.

It never crossed my mind that he was someplace where he just shouldn't be. I just didn't care, or I wasn't thinking clearly. Instead, I just stared impassively into the truck and said, "Hi, Larry."

"Are you feeling OK, Larry?" he replied. "You're not looking so good today. You look a little bit green!"

"Yeah, I feel a little bit green," I admitted. "I don't know what it is. I went to bed feeling OK last night, but I feel like I'm coming down with something this morning. Given my druthers, I'd stay in bed today, but that's not really an option. I've got to get in to Cedar Lakes to start my route."

"Well, tell you what," he said with a grin. "I can't get you all the way in to Cedars, but why don't you toss your pack into the back and I'll give you a ride up the ridge and down to Grassy Brook. That'll save you a couple of miles of walking, anyway."

I didn't need to be asked twice. Instead, I hoisted my load into the back of the pickup truck and accepted the ride. For a fleeting moment or two, I thought about the appropriateness of my actions, as I wasn't supposed to be doing this. However, I didn't think too hard, knowing darn well that it was a lot easier riding than climbing and that someone in the DEC must have given him the key to the gate in the first place. In other words, my conscience lost that battle rather easily.

Getting the lift helped cut down my time, and I made it to the dam at Cedar Lakes by early afternoon. A group of three campers from Gloversville were in the lean-to, so I decided to pitch my tent nearby and see how I felt. Normally, I would head down the lake and check out the other lean-tos on Cedars and then backtrack to camp for the night. But not tonight. This was as far as I was going.

As I set up my tent (even that felt tiring), I spoke with the campers in the lean-to. One of them had met me on a previous occasion, although I did not remember speaking to him. I looked at them through dull eyes as they prepared to do some late afternoon fishing.

"I've got an extra line if you'd like to give it a shot," said one of them as he tied a knot onto a lure. "Catching a nice native brookie might make you feel a little better. At least it will taste better than that stuff I saw you eating last time I was here. It looked like you were rehydrating a sponge!"

I politely declined and went off to lie down in my tent, all the while feeling worse as the afternoon progressed. By dinner time, I knew I was running a fever. I decided that I wasn't hungry enough to warrant preparing supper for myself, which was highly unusual for me, as I always had a pretty good appetite.

The campers in the lean-to took an active interest in my plight and offered to provide some ready-made chow.

"Hey, we got some of the good stuff," said Mick, the sportsman who claimed that we'd met the previous year. "I bet you don't have any of this in your pack!"

As he spoke, he unwrapped a heavily dressed package clad in several layers of foil. Inside was a small pile of fresh steaks, which had been frozen solid prior to their hike in to preserve them until the end of the day. This was something that I noticed on a regular basis; fishermen and local campers tended to carry in much better food than those hikers who had to worry about weight and distance. In this case, they were prepared for a feast. In another bag were six or eight large potatoes, a few red onions, and a half-dozen ears of corn. It was impressive.

True to the form displayed by other local woodsmen, they built a rather massive pile of sawed and split wood, which would serve to provide a raging fire late into the night. Their potatoes hit the coals first, while their corn and steaks were given a much later start.

It was a late dinner, and the temperature was starting to drop already by the time we sat down to eat. I had accepted their invitation, albeit with the caveat that I probably couldn't eat much. I felt pretty useless as I sat in the front of the lean-to, watching the activity going on around me. My normal practice would have been to help get wood and then prepare my own meal. However, tonight I just snuggled deeper into my wool jacket, sluggishly watching everyone else do the chores. They all recognized my condition, though, and understood how I felt.

As expected, I had a difficult time working up any sort of an appetite. The plate that one of the campers handed me was laden with a beautiful looking piece of seared steak, along with a perfectly roasted ear of corn. Just looking at them would have normally induced waves of hunger in me, especially at the end of a long day in the woods. Instead, all I could do was take a few bites of the meat, chewing noncommittally as I watched the rest of the group. No matter what, I couldn't do justice to their culinary skills, so I decided to call it an early night and turn in.

I spent that night in an uncomfortable slumber, turning, feeling chilled, then sweating, then chilled again. When morning came, I felt as though I hadn't been to bed yet. I knew that my fever had climbed higher during the night, and I was still getting worse. I decided to call my friend, Peter Gloo, the forest fire observer up on Wakely Mountain and have him relay to my boss, Tom Eakin, the message that I wasn't going to stay on schedule this week.

"Do you need any help?" Pete replied, the concern reflected in his voice. "I could call Tom and have him meet you in his truck and give you a ride out."

"No, that's OK, at least for now," I said. "I don't think I need any help, but I'm going to stay right here at Cedar Lakes Dam for at least the next day and see how I feel." My schedule had me moving past West Lake and on to Sampson the next day. However, I knew that wasn't going to happen.

"OK, but keep in touch, and let me know how you are doing, OK?" Pete said. It was so nice to have him on the tower, as it was one of the only radios I could hit from my remote location, and even then, there were only a few spots that would work. It required a lot of luck and the right conditions.

It was also nice to have had a group of friendly local folks staying with me in case I needed help. The steak dinner hadn't hurt either, even if I couldn't finish much of it. Unfortunately, they were leaving that day around noon, having spent only one night in the woods. I watched them pack up their things as I stood lethargically next to my tent. Despite my official duties, I wanted nothing more than to crawl back into my sleeping bag and drift off to sleep. I had no energy to do anything beyond that.

At this point, I hadn't eaten a real meal in quite some time.

Knowing that I should put something into my stomach, I reached into my food bag and extracted a summer sausage, a bag of sunflower seeds, and some fruit drink mix. Hardly a delicacy when compared to the steak of the previous evening but still a tasty treat.

I sat down on the bench of the old picnic table that was situated next to the lean-to, my boots crunching in the soil. It was the only sound to be heard now that the campers had left. I cut off a slice of the summer sausage, savoring the seasoning as it went down. Wow, I thought, this stuff is pretty darn good! I gulped a little of the fruit drink, but basically ignored the sunflower seeds because the sausage tasted so good. I quickly grabbed my knife and cut off a second slice of the preserved meat, even thicker than the first. Not bad at all!

For the first time in a couple of days, my appetite felt reinvigorated. It was almost as though that part of me was saying, "Here I am...feed me!" And "feed me" I did, with slice after slice of the sausage, sometimes with a piece of bread, sometimes all by itself. It all tasted wonderful, at least for the first five or six slices, and then the taste became very bland, as though I was eating something without flavor at all. But still, as though hypnotized, I kept eating, feeling my stomach filling until it was overextended. Why I did this is beyond my comprehension, but I think I was simply in a mindless trance, pushing the stuff into my mouth.

Suddenly, the summer sausage took another turn for the worse and tasted simply noxious. I looked down at the last half-eaten slice, sitting on the table next to my canteen, and I knew that I'd never be able to swallow it, even if offered a healthy reward. It didn't even look appealing, and I just wanted to get rid of the stuff. Grabbing it by its outer skin, I reared back and launched a high-arcing shot into the middle of Cedar Lake outlet. I'm sure that every single catfish and crawdad in the lake followed it down to the bottom. As far as I was concerned, they could have it.

My sleeping bag was still beckoning to me, so I decided to heed its call. Even though it was only early afternoon, I crawled inside my tent and zipped up the flaps. I was closed for business. Things must have gotten pretty bad after that, because my memory of the next two days is really blurred. I am fairly certain that I saw my partner, John Wood, as he came through, although I cannot honestly recall speaking to him. I also remember hearing another group coming by the lean-to and setting up camp, but I stayed inside the tent for most of that day and the following night.

When I awoke the next morning, the group had already packed up and left, but I remained in my bag, drifting back and forth into a state of semi-consciousness. Even when I did try getting up, my joints ached and my head hurt in a most uncomfortable way. It was not good.

I also discovered that summer sausage tastes a lot better going down than it does coming back up. Enough said.

I never did make it down into the West Canadas that weekend, staying instead in that one spot for the entire week. I accepted another meal later in the week from a pair of hikers who were going from Piseco to Blue Mountain Lake, traversing some of the most beautiful territory our Park has to offer. They arrived at the lean-to on Monday afternoon, planning to spend the night there before heading north the following morning. I would be heading out of the woods myself that day, but going the opposite direction, southeast towards Perkins Clearing. Even though they were a bit limited in their stores, they insisted on preparing an extra meal for me, as I was still showing the signs of my flu-like illness. They cooked up a large pot of what I'd have to describe as a goulash, or beef stew, which they served over a bed of rice. It was delicious. It was also something that I'd never eaten in the woods (I was doing a lot of that this week), having come from a specialty camping store in Vermont.

Given their need to re-supply, it was very generous of them to offer me a meal as they did. However, I didn't feel too bad about accepting their offerings, as I was able to give them a fair amount of the contents of my own food bag, which I had ignored for most of the week. Almost everything, including bread, cheese, noodles, granola bars, and some dehydrated dinner packages were transferred into their packs as they prepared to move on the next morning.

By the time Tuesday morning rolled around, I was feeling well enough to put on my pack, although my legs felt a bit shaky. As for the rest of my regular patrol route, it remained unpatrolled for the week. For all I knew, the entire West Canada Lakes Wilderness Area could have fallen off the Earth and into a giant abyss. I didn't care. I'd be back the following week. It was OK.

I thank my lucky stars that that was the only time I was ever forced into neglecting the duties of my job. (Perhaps "neglect" is too strong a word, but I did feel quite badly about the situation, even though there was very little I could do about it.) I am also thankful that in three years, neither I nor any of my partners ever sustained a serious illness or injury.

I think back on that week and appreciate the concern and assistance given to me by a wide variety of people, from the local "old-timers" to the first-time through hikers. They all wanted to help, and I feel grateful to all of them. In the remote regions of the backcountry, people need to rely on other people when they get into a jam. Though I was never really in trouble, it was nice to know that I could count on these total strangers in a time of need.

They say that hindsight is 20-20, and in retrospect, there are two things that I would have changed about that malady-filled week in the woods. The first is that I would have brought in some medicine to help with the fever, aches, and pains brought on by the flu. I never could have known how much that might have helped to alleviate my symptoms that week, and I made a mental note to add such pharmaceuticals to my first aid kit for future use.

The second had to do with that summer sausage, which I vowed to never, EVER carry in my pack again.

—14—

Out of Place

Living back in the woods, far away from roads, cars, stores, and people for days and weeks on end, can do strange things to a person. Not that these things are bad; several of them are actually very good. For example, I found that often I would start to tune in much better to my surroundings and notice things that I just wouldn't have noticed before I moved into the woods. Sounds and subtle changes in scenery are amplified, as though your senses are put into overdrive. It doesn't happen overnight, but the change is significant and noticeable.

This made it seem even more noticeable when something truly out of place appeared, sometimes seemingly out of nowhere. It might be something as casual as the approach of a large log floating down to the dam on Cedar Lakes, or the sudden appearance of supersonic Air Force fighter jets, screaming over the landscape in a low-level training run.

Huh? Air Force jets in the wilderness? Unfortunately, the answer to this was yes. Jet fighter training flights took off from Griffiss Air Force Base, located to the southwest of our territory, in Rome, New York. To say that this happened on a frequent enough basis to ruin anyone's backcountry experience would be false. They didn't. At most, I would see them once every few weeks.

It was always interesting to see the changes that happened in the woods in the moments before these huge war birds actually appeared, because before you saw them, you heard them. And before you heard them, you could actually *feel* them. It was as though there was a low, inaudible rumble that moved the ground in a silent, rapid shaking motion. Birds squawked and launched themselves from their roosts in the trees. Squirrels headed up trees while chipmunks scurried for their holes.

Then came the noise. It began as a high pitched whine. It increased in volume rapidly and decreased in pitch, going from barely audible to deafening in a matter of ten to fifteen seconds. Making matters even more interesting (and much louder) is the fact that they tended to fly at very low altitudes, simulating the moves that they'd fly in an actual combat scenario. This could serve to hide both the noise and the appearance of the aircraft until it was almost on top of you.

By the time the planes passed overhead, often two or three together in close formation, the noise of the awe-inspiring sight was truly shocking. The ground rumbled, and everyone, and I mean *everyone*, who could see them would stop and watch until they flew from view. Then the sight and sound died down and disappeared within a matter of seconds. Gone, with a rapid return to total silence.

There were some folks who were bothered by the appearance of these planes and claimed that they should not be allowed to conduct training runs over designated wilderness areas. After all, if the old timer pilots were no longer allowed to land their aircraft on these lakes, why should the military be able to conduct fly-overs? However, those rules only applied to actually *landing* on the lakes, and so far none of the supersonic aircraft had ever appeared overhead carrying a pair of water landing skids!

During my months in the Pillsbury Mountain fire tower, I saw these jets a bit more often, as I had a much greater field of view that could reach from the High Peaks in the north to the Green Mountains of Vermont. So although they might appear more frequently and even "buzz" the tower, I always knew when they were coming. Still, they were a strange part of my life in the woods that always fascinated me and yanked me (forcefully at times) out of my element.

Not all of the unusual sightings in the woods were so dramatic or loud. One of the more pleasant events I stumbled upon was at the lean-to up on Cedar River Flow, just a few miles away from the Wakely Dam. This spot was the northern-most point of my patrols, and I never stayed there overnight. It was a pretty location, although it never received much in the way of use.

One unusual feature about this lean-to was that it could be reached fairly quickly from Wakely Dam on the Moose River Plains. It was an easy, flat hike, which meant that those who did go there were recreational users who wanted to carry their beer and other refreshments into the woods. The story was still told about the bunch of hippies in the late 1960s that carried several gallons of brightly colored paint into the woods and converted the lean-to into a psychedelic love shelter. According to the tale, the structure was torn down and a new natural log replacement was built in its place. I could never verify that this really happened, but it made for an interesting story.

Regardless of its history, I never dallied there for long. My schedule for the day was to patrol the Northville-Lake Placid Trail from Cedar Lakes to this northern site and then return to Cedars in a straight line. I would occasionally stop there for lunch, but nothing more. I was rather ambivalent about this particular day in my schedule. I liked it because I didn't need to bring along my big heavy Kelty pack. I could leave it behind at Cedar Lakes and just bring a day pack. However, I didn't like it because I preferred actually going somewhere, ending up at a different destination rather than just doing a down and back pattern.

Anyhow, on one memorable afternoon, as I strolled down the gentle slope towards the back of the creekside lean-to, I thought I heard something out of place. I was still some distance from the winding river and the log structure, but I knew that I heard something. Someone must be in there, perhaps playing a radio.

Moving closer, I started picking out the sounds of stringed instruments. It was tough to tell what, exactly, I was listening to, but it sounded nice. Also, the closer I got, the less it sounded like a radio and the more it sounded like live music.

Rounding the corner of the lean-to, I was greeted by the sight of seven young men and women, spread out in various positions both seated and standing, the majority of them picking and strumming some type of instrument. There were two guitars, one violin, one mandolin, and one long (very long!) instrument that was making the sounds of a base. This last instrument truly baffled me, because it was not the big and bulky hulk that defined the typical base or cello, but it did produce very deep rich sounds which complemented the other instruments.

There was a definite drop in volume as I made my appearance, probably startling these woodsy musicians as I made my way towards the ensemble. However, I immediately gave them a big smile, accompanied with a conductor's movement of my hands to encourage them to continue. Several of them returned my smile and continued on with their piece.

Two members of the party, who appeared to be of college age, were not playing anything. Instead, they had spread a red tablecloth out across the floor of the lean-to. They extracted a stack of clear plastic cups from a paper bag and commenced pouring quantities of red wine from a large green bottle.

I removed my pack and sat down on a makeshift bench that was placed in front of the shelter, hoping that the group would not mind my presence. Even in the city, these kids would have sounded pretty good. In the woods, their music was positively enchanting, and I sat there enthralled, soaking up the sounds.

Often times the presence of alcohol in the woods spelled trouble. However, in this case it was merely a refreshment, to be served as an accompaniment to the concert. They had obviously spent a lot of time practicing their pieces, because I did not see anything in the way of music books. I refused a cup of wine and was on my way within about thirty minutes, but it was a purely joyful sound that stayed with me the rest of the day. What an afternoon! I would never again run into something like this, and it would remain forever as my one and only concert on the creek.

Out of place occurrences didn't have to be anything as extravagant as a five-piece string group. On the contrary, some of them were as simple as the sight of the electrical outlet which some hiker (possessing a great sense of humor!) had screwed into the side of the third Cedar Lake lean-to. Miles from the nearest genuine electrical source, this piece of hardware caused me to break into laughter each time I stayed there.

Other pieces of out-of-place equipment in the deep woods dated back to the days of the hunting camps that dotted the landscape around the smaller lakes. The trail that led past Pillsbury Lake on the way to Sampson Lake passed several of these relics. It was always sad to have to walk past the shell of an old refrigerator, which had been dragged out of a plywood structure on the trail that branched off to Whitney Lake. I tried pulling it out of the line of sight on one summer afternoon, only to discover that there were numerous hornet's nests affixed to the lining inside. I escaped without getting stung, although I resolved to wait until the onset of winter to finish the job.

There were other items to be found, such as the remains of an old jalopy that had been pulled off the trail to Whitney Lake in the days when the path must have been much wider. It was rusted to the point of dilapidation, and it was no longer possible even to identify the type of vehicle it had been. Indeed, many people who passed by never noticed it nestled down in the over-growth. I often wished that I too did not see these discarded remnants of the old camps, for they scarred the natural beauty of the woods and somehow made the entire area seem less remote.

Not all of the modern items carried in by our hikers were eyesores, and sometimes I was pleasantly surprised by what people would decide to carry into the woods. On one not-so-pleasant August afternoon, I was making the trip from Sampson Lake through the West Canadas in route to the Beaver Pond lean-to on Cedar Lakes. It was cold and it had been raining, which made for a messy start to the day. (Many people living in warmer parts of the country have a hard time picturing a cold day in August. However, I have experienced many days in the Adirondack woods when the temperature dropped to the point where snow felt probable.)

Because it was the middle of the week and the trails were relatively empty, I felt little need to get going early. I stayed in my sleeping bag until mid-morning, then arose and fixed myself a hot breakfast of oatmeal and freeze-dried omelet. I very seldom cooked a big breakfast like that, which put me even further behind schedule for the day.

The walk from Sampson Lake to the junction of the Northville-Lake Placid trail is about three miles long, and I plodded along slowly, needing a full hour to cover the distance. Never a really fast walker unless required, I felt my muscles and bones slowed even more by the cool temperatures and the general wetness of the soil. I could see my breath in the air ahead of me, and I moved ahead in a dreamlike state.

Reaching the Placid Trail, I turned north and headed over West Canada Creek toward West Lake. In addition to the cold temperature, I just felt grumbly. I had no reason for feeling that way, but I was not in a great mood. I'd read that honey bees were often hard to work with on days when the weather was nasty, and I felt that I understood their sentiment.

Re-entering the woods past the creek, I continued north until I crested the small hill that marked the descent to the South Lake lean-to. As I did so, the clouds suddenly parted and a brilliant sun burst through the opening. As the skies continued to clear, a patch of blue expanded overhead, and bright rays of light came slashing though the trees, illuminating everything in a golden glow. In that instant, both the air temperature and my spirits were raised by at least twenty degrees.

Rejuvenated by the sunlight, I quickened my step, which now felt as though it had some bounce in it. Amazing what a little change in climate can do! I covered the final few hundred yards to the South Lake lean-to without seemingly touching the ground. I was flying.

Then I came to a sudden stop. What in the world was going on here? Looking ahead of me, which would have been the east end of South Lake, was as bizarre a sight as I had ever seen in the woods. The wind was whipping up the cool air in a consistently strong breeze. And taking advantage of those winds were a number of kites, streaming away at full mast as they danced over the lake. Two of these kites were identical except in color; one was red and the other was blue. They were fairly traditional models that resembled a flying bird, with a wide wingspan and a long tail streaming from the back end. The third kite was a green creation that looked as through three or four kites had been attached together. Unlike the steady flight path of the first two kites, this one was flying zigzag patterns back and forth along the shoreline at a much lower altitude. I believe it was being steered by its owner, although I am not a kite enthusiast and know very little about the hobby.

I sauntered over to talk to the three gentlemen who were standing on the sandy beach of South Lake, each tending their own string and intently sailing their kites. Residents of Albany, they were in the woods for three days of relaxation and nothing else. I learned this from Mark, the owner of the green multi-kite, as he was the closest member of the party to the trail.

"Oh, we just thought it might be a fun thing to do for an hour or so," he explained. As he did so, he sent his kite into another series of aeronautic acrobatics. "We brought them here right out of the store and put them together in the lean-to. But those other guys got the easy end of the deal," he said, nodding at his friends. "All they had to do was 'Insert pole A into sleeve B.' I had to actually cut the paper and glue the parts together. You ever try using crazy glue in a lean-to?"

I had to agree with him that no, I had never tried to assemble a kite in such a remote part of the woods either, although I did admire his work. I have no idea how long they stuck to their pursuit, because I left them after only conversing for a very brief time. I returned to the trail, which paralleled the beach as it moved over the bridge and back into the woods just south of John's caretaker's station. Glancing back over my shoulder one last time, I got a final view of the three colorful kites, waving back and forth in the glorious blue sky. To the best of my knowledge, they may be the only kites ever to have flown above the waters of the West Canada Lakes.

Other things that could catch my attention were the presence or signs of an animal species that did not normally reside in the area. The obvious examples were mammals, such as the visiting moose that passed through the southeast corner of our territory. In other cases, in might be something much more elusive, such as a species of bird that adds a new call to the otherwise familiar background noise.

Such was the case one morning in late August. I was in the process of getting my pack together to hit the trail when I stopped dead in my tracks. From the tall ridge in back of the Cedar Lakes lean-to #1 by the dam I heard a noise that was simultaneously familiar and foreign.

"Gobble, gobble, gobble, gobble, gobble, gobble, gobble, gobble, gobble!" A high pitched call that decreased in pitch slightly as it progressed, it was long, lasting approximately five to seven seconds, and it was loud.

Well, not much doubt what kind of bird made that noise. It

was obviously a wild turkey, probably either perched in a tree or stalking the woods under the brush up on the ridge. But where the heck had it come from? We didn't have turkeys in our area, and to the best of my knowledge they didn't live in this part of the state.

"Gobble, gobble, gobble, gobble, gobble, gobble, gobble, gobble, gobble!" There it went again, clear as a bell, seemingly calling to me. "Hey...Ranger Larry...gobble, gobble, gobble, here I am, come up and get me!"

I continued to pack, pushing my food sack and cooking pot into the upper part of my pack, finishing with my wool jacket and sleeping roll. As I did, I heard it again.

"Gobble, gobble, gobble, gobble, gobble." However, this bird sounded different. Its call was not as loud as the first, and it wasn't as long.

Now don't get me wrong; I'm no slouch when it comes to identifying animals in the woods. I'm fairly good with mammals, and my knowledge of invertebrates (especially insects) is pretty darned good. But I am not an ornithologist. I do not know the subtleties of bird calls, nor can I tell you what species call at what times of day and for what reasons. All I knew was that the bird I heard was a turkey. Hold the stuffing!

Determined to find the source of the calls, I turned away from the lean-to and started walking as silently as possible up the hill. There were no other campers in the area, and the morning was very still. Since that time, I've read many articles about the keen senses (especially sight) of the wild turkey, although I didn't know about that at the time. Had I realized this, I would never have bothered even dreaming of walking up and finding these birds. But at the time I didn't know about their amazing abilities, so off I went.

I used the foot path to the outhouse to cover the first hundred feet in order to keep down the noise. (There were no leaves and sticks to crunch on the path.) As I passed the outhouse, I picked out my projected route, mentally planning each step to avoid anything that could make a sound. I treaded lightly, silently, like a wisp of smoke floating through the sparse underbrush leading up the hill. As I moved ahead, I began to crouch slightly, still making good time. I felt like a skilled predator, silently stalking its prey.

I guess the first sign that something was wrong was that I kept hearing the turkeys calling out loudly as I moved ahead. These Adirondack turkeys were either very brave or very dumb, because they certainly weren't fleeing.

"Gobble, gobble, gobble, gobble, gobble, gobble, gobble, gobble, gobble!" went the first bird, loud and strong. I could almost see the feathered creature, bobbing its head as it walked, foraging for food in the brush.

"Gobble, gobble, gobble, gobble, gobble," came the reply of the smaller (or younger, or more timid?) bird, answering moments later.

This was getting exciting. I knew that I was getting closer, because the calls were now being accompanied by sounds in the brush. The sounds of scuffling and movement could plainly be heard in a dip that was just beyond the crest of a ridge that hid my goal from view. However, I would not be deterred. Soon I would be on my quarry, able to see these beautiful birds. I crept ahead stealthily.

"Gobble, gobble, gobble, gobble, gobble, gobble, gobble, gobble, gobble!" called the first bird.

"Gobble, gobble, gobble, gobble," followed the second.

With a final silent burst of speed, I crested the ridge and pounced into the depression. There, just beyond a patch of thick, young striped maple trees was a low-slung blue tarp, stretched tightly above two sleeping bags and a large ground cloth. On the ground was a man with his teenaged son, each with a round turkey call instrument at the ready.

"No, John, you've almost got it, but not quite. It's got to go a little further back in your mouth, like this," the father demon-strated. Once again, the call pierced the silence of the woods.

"Gobble, gobble, gobble, gobble, gobble, gobble, gobble, gobble, gobble!" came the realistic call. "And don't be afraid to make that call just a little bit louder and a little bit longer. You want to sound like a really <u>big</u> tom!"

—15—

Fighting the Losing Battle

Ever since I worked in the West Canada Lakes, I have had great respect for *Castor canadensis*. For those unable to recognize the name, this is the scientific appellation for the North American beaver. A native to the Eastern United States, the beaver has found a home in almost all backcountry ponds and lakes and is responsible for the creation of many new, smaller bodies of water.

Beavers are actually a larger animal than most people realize. They vary in size between twenty-four and thirty-six inches long, with a twelve- to eighteen-inch tail. They have weighed in as heavy as seventy pounds, with a few claims going much higher, which is larger than many of the other animals in those areas. They are, in fact, the largest rodent in North America. Beavers have large upper incisors which grow continuously. It is these teeth that are used to gnaw through hardwoods such as maple and oak.

Watching these highly adapted animals go about their daily routines, you can really understand the origin of the expression "busy as a beaver." These creatures are seemingly never at rest. Whether cutting down trees for building material, shoring up weak points in a dam, or focusing on their home life inside their well-built lodges, beavers are always on the go.

Beavers are appreciated on different levels by different groups of individuals, depending on how they come into contact with one another. Hikers who are looking to see the local wildlife as they pass through the area always appreciate a visit from one or more of these critters, especially if they can watch them in action, carrying sticks back to their lodge. It's always a good show, and children (if tagging along) have a great time trying to hear the trademark tail slap signifying danger in the area. However, those same hikers are a bit less enthusiastic when they have to traverse a lengthy stretch of trail that has been flooded due to beaver activity. Suddenly, the very same animals that they deemed cute back at the campsite have migrated over the line to being a nuisance.

One of the most appreciative fans of the beaver is the local population of trappers, who benefit from the high-quality pelts that they can collect during the winter trapping season. Beavers, whose pelts can add a significant figure to the annual take of a trapper, are plentiful throughout the region.

Although I discussed trapping with a few of the local sports-men, I never knew anyone besides John who actually trapped back there. Then again, this is not a group of people I would be likely to meet, as they tended to stay away from the frequently-used trails and shelters used by the hikers. Trapping is a cold and lonely winter pursuit that lends itself to the rugged individualist, and these hardy woodsmen did not interact with the normal recreational visitors.

Another group of people who appreciated seeing the local beavers out and about were the photographers. Very few hikers brought extensive photographic equipment back into the deep woods, as it added both bulk and weight to any pack. And when you add in the extra dimensions of a tripod, light meters, and the rest, it all could amount to a full backpack of its own. However, some aspiring wildlife photographers did occasionally make an appearance with a full kit bag, and most of them spent some time focusing on one of the many local beaver lodges.

Very few of these visitors, however, photographed these aquatic rodents as frequently as my friend Al, who visited me on a couple of occasions during the summer months. Not that Al had a fancy camera, or even cared about the quality of his prints. But Al loved taking pictures of beaver lodges, and he took advantage of every chance he got to shoot each and every lodge in the area.

The two of us would hike the Perkins Clearing trail from the clearing into Cedar Lakes, and Al always stopped to take photographs at least a dozen times. If a beaver happened to show itself, he would dutifully record its activities as it swam around the pond and returned home. There were times when I thought that he had enough action photos to stack them up and make a flip-through movie! But no harm was done, except to delay our arrival by an hour or so, while the beaver population of each lodge was duly photographed for posterity.

One other useful function that beavers performed (albeit unintentionally) was to provide numerous hikers in our territory with really nice walking sticks. They gnaw the branches off of larger limbs, which they then proceed to peel and size before weaving them into their dam or lodge. The results of this work are nicely sized, peeled sticks that are decorated with symmetrical teeth markings along their length. The tops and bottoms show the characteristic chopping and cutting bites that beavers use to detach limbs from the rest of the tree.

I never used one of these ready-made walking sticks until my third year on the job. When I lost my usual stick during my final month in the woods, I simply reached into a new dam that was under construction at the south end of Beaver Pond and extracted a single stick. Perfect! It was just the right length and thickness, and it fit my hand perfectly. I doubt that my friends in the beaver lodge would have approved, but it was a rather minor bit of theft, so I didn't give it a second thought. Instead, I allowed it to dry, and then applied a few coats of lacquer to give it a shine and a layer of protection. It turned out beautifully, and I still use that same stick to this day.

Beaver dams varied greatly in size throughout our area, depending upon the length of waterway that they needed to plug. Some of these, such as the one at the outlet of Beaver Pond into Cedar Lakes, were only a short span and could be built relatively quickly. However, there were some dams that reached truly astounding proportions. One such structure was built south of my regular territory, near the Hamilton Pond lean-to. This dam was solely responsible for the creation of a large pond which rerouted the Northville-Lake Placid trail for a good quarter mile.

The dam itself was forty to fifty feet long and six to eight feet tall. I marveled at its size and strength and at the idea that any group of creatures such as beavers could have completed such an engineering feat. Rather than walk below their dam on the old eroded trail, I chose to walk across its top, which was as strong as any bridge built by a trail crew. My only complaint with this "bridge" was that the beavers had failed to build a hand rail spanning the length of the structure. I had no doubt that had the beavers chosen to do so, they could have completed this feature as well!

In any case, by the time I had completed my first year in the woods, I was highly respectful of the building capabilities of these animals. They seemed to be able to build just about anything they wanted, regardless of how much time and effort humans put into preventing them from doing so. I learned this the hard way one week when I volunteered to help John clear one of these dams that had been giving us problems. Halfway between Mud Lake and West Lake was a very wet, swampy area with a decent sized pond, which had an outlet into West Lake. The pond received most of its water through the drain-off from Mud Lake, although I had never bothered to wade through the mud to actually observe this.

Mud Lake itself is a very shallow, muddy-bottomed body of water that serves as home to a great many species of birds and animals. In addition to beavers, I have seen otters, deer, and pine martens in and around the lake. A large nest near the northern shore of the lake serves as home to a great blue heron, which flaps its giant wings and goes airborne at the first sight of human intruders. The outlet from Mud Lake drains southward and splits into two parts. A smaller trickle of water drains west and feeds the east end of South Lake under the long, wooden foot bridge. But most of the water that flows from Mud Lake heads southwest, forming the origins of the famous West Canada Creek.

The trail from Cedar Lakes to the caretaker's cabin on West Lake (which has since been rerouted) used to cross directly over the outlet of the small pond sitting between Mud Lake and West Lake. Proceeding west across the outlet, the path crossed a meadow by the old helicopter landing pad, which was about three hundred yards from John's cabin. That trail had been in trouble for years, as the beavers had apparently decided that the water level of the pond was not quite as high as they wanted. To raise it, they had built a series of small dams across the outlet stream, which rapidly pushed the waterline up into the meadow. As the water rose, some hikers had taken a bunch of boards that were left over from the old helicopter landing pad and constructed a makeshift walkway over the standing water in the trail. (The helicopter pad was a relic from the days when many of the caretaker's supplies were flown into the woods. It had since fallen into a state of disrepair and was no longer usable.) This walkway sufficed, especially if you had good balance, but anyone who fell off the boards would go calf-deep in water. It was not a good solution.

One day in mid-summer, John asked my assistance to help him clear one of the dams from the outlet.

"It doesn't seem like that should be very difficult, John," I commented. We were sitting in the front room of his cabin, watching the mercury on his antique thermometer creep into the low 80s. "I'll stay here on West tonight instead of going down to Sampson. That way we can get out there early and wrap it up by noon."

John got a good laugh out of that one. He knew that I didn't enjoy going over to Sampson Lake to stay the night. Sampson was a lonely place that seldom received visitors. I often felt that my time and efforts were wasted whenever I visited that part of the woods.

"Oh, we'll be done by noon? Good!" John responded, his quiet sarcasm coming through clearly. "I think you're going to be in for a surprise tomorrow. But never mind; I'll let you be the judge." He had obviously decided that I, with my youthful ignorance, would get enough of an education without any additional elaboration. I would learn about beaver dams from on-the-job experience.

I agreed to meet John at his cabin at eight o'clock the next morning. He asked me to meet him there instead of at the dam so that I could carry some equipment for him. This also surprised me, as I couldn't picture what we'd need in the way of supplies, except perhaps a saw for cutting some of the larger limbs out of the way.

It was only when I saw the stockpile of tools and devices that I began to get suspicious. It was positively scary. Shovels and saws, crowbars, and skid devices that I had never seen before. All of these were stacked neatly in a pile in the back of the clearing, ready to be carried down to the site of the dams. My first impression was that John was using a bit of overkill on this project. However, I knew John well enough to realize that he would *never* bring along a tool unless he was pretty certain he'd use it. Not that John was lazy in any way; he was one of the most hardworking men I'd ever met, but he also believed in conservation of energy whenever possible.

We headed off down the trail, following it to the marsh

before cutting off and following the outlet creek downstream. After about a quarter mile, we arrived at a well-constructed dam that was about twenty to twenty-five feet across and four feet tall. Its finely meshed stick and limb construction was very efficient, as evidenced by the lack of leakage on the downstream side. I couldn't begin to fathom the number of individual trips that these beavers had made back and forth from the pond and woods where they had retrieved this material. Plus, with all the cutting and peeling of the branches and the weaving of the dam itself, it was a project that defied my imagination.

John started at one side of the dam while I started at the other. We knew that we'd have to help each other a lot, especially when a piece called for heavy lifting or pulling. But for the most part, it reminded me of "reverse engineering" a piece of equipment, which means taking it apart in the same way that it was built. Branches and roots and trunks were all patched together tightly and sometimes had to be removed in a particular order to make any progress. From time to time, we needed to use the crowbar to lift heavier pieces out of the muck, as they had become waterlogged over time. It was hot, tiring work, and my shirt was soon stuck to my body with sweat under the midday sun.

"We'll know we're making progress when we start to see a lot of water passing through," said John, wiping his brow with his handkerchief. "These beavers are clever builders and they know how to plug up a creek. You'll see a lot more of their tricks as we get further into this thing."

I wasn't sure that I was looking forward to that, as I was being physically tested already. I was also curious about how much we would really affect the level of the marsh by removing this one dam. It seemed to me that there was one heck of a lot of water back there causing the trail to be flooded. I pictured it taking a good week or two for the water level to come back down to dry ground.

As we removed the peeled sticks and branches from the dam,

we threw them to the side of the creek banks, where they grew into an impressive-sized pile of their own. I wouldn't have given that a second thought until I saw John loading a large stack of them onto a sheet metal skid and start pulling it into the woods some distance away. I didn't ask what he was doing, as John knew a lot more about the practical side of woodsmanship than did I. But when he returned, which was several minutes later, he saw the questioning look in my eye.

"You've got to get rid of all that stuff, and you've got to hide it out of view. Otherwise that beaver family would just take it from the creek bank and stick it right back into the dam."

"Wow," I said, "That wouldn't be good. They probably work longer hours than us, too!"

John took a moment to wipe the sweat from his brow again, grunting as he did. He never appeared to enjoy hard labor, but he could keep going all day with a boundless energy that always seemed to flow from his sinewy body.

"Somehow, I think they'll find it anyway and end up dragging the pile of it back down here. Kind of makes you wonder, y'know; does this all make sense? We spend a full day out here killing ourselves so that the hikers don't get wet feet while walking through the wilderness. And then, after it's all said and done, the damn beavers just drag the same stuff back here in a week or two, and presto, dam rebuilt! I'll bet the whole bunch of them are just sitting in their lodge right now, laughing at us as we try to take this thing down."

John broke into a gentle laugh at the thought of being observed by the beaver clan. I didn't always agree with everything that John said, but I had to admit that this struck a humorous chord in me as well.

By the time we stopped for lunch, we were well into the process. We had lowered the top of the dam by at least a foot and had also loosened up the edges to the point where there were some major leaks through the span. The flow of water was hardly a torrent, but it was at least a start.

John provided lunch back at his cabin, which was a bit of a treat. After all, he had a propane-powered refrigerator which he occasionally stocked with good things brought in from Speculator. This included items that I just couldn't keep in my pack, such as fresh lettuce and tomatoes. We sat inside, away from the drone of the mosquitoes, blackflies, and deerflies. That alone was quite a luxury.

As John puttered around in his pantry putting together sandwiches and iced tea, I wondered aloud about our progress.

"Do you think that if we just left that dam as it is, the water level would stay where it is? That makeshift walkway of lumber is pretty easy to walk over, and it's several inches above the water. Maybe we'd be OK just leaving it alone."

John looked out the window as he considered the matter, his eyes casting a thoughtful glance in the direction of the lake.

"No, I don't think they'll stop until the whole thing is under water again, and maybe not even then. It almost seems like they want to connect the pond up to Mud Lake. Lord knows they've got the energy to do it."

I considered what he was saying as I took an exploratory bite into the sandwich that John had placed in front of me. Closing my eyes, I bit with ecstasy into the simple bologna on white bread with lettuce, tomato, and mayonnaise. It's hard to believe how good something so simple like that can taste, especially with the lettuce so cold and crisp and the mayonnaise providing some additional moisture to the stack. After all, I had been living on a staple diet of canned ham on old rye bread, served warm out of the pack. Or, when I needed a break, I could always turn to peanut butter and jelly, which had also grown old on my palate. This was better than good; it was absolutely great!

As I chewed my food, I waited for John to continue on with his thoughts about the prospects of winning the struggle with the beavers. He had a rather somber look about him, which reflected his opinion that this would be a long, hard-fought battle. However, as tough an adversary as the beaver could be, I knew that John was willing to go the distance, too. I had witnessed him in action as he fought the red squirrels, which seemed to enjoy gnawing holes through the insulation of the single copper phone line that ran from Perkins Clearing to his caretaker's cabin. No matter how many holes they chewed, allowing water to get into the line and causing a short circuit, John was always willing to track them down and repair them.

After a short rest, we sauntered back down to the dam and picked up on our work. Some clouds had moved over the sun, making it feel a bit cooler, which was a good thing, because the further down we excavated, the more surprises we found. Beavers don't only build with sticks and branches; they also employ sturdier materials such as rocks and packed mud. At times, we needed the crowbar to pry some fairly good-sized rocks out of the way. It left me wondering how the heck these creatures could get them there in the first place. It is true that they are big, strong animals with disproportionately large heads and teeth, but how could they transport these rocks from the creek bed and lift them up to plug holes in the middle of the dam? Perhaps they did it using teamwork, or maybe it was some other trick that they had learned over the years. Regardless, they never stopped working long enough to tell me about it, so I never learned how it was accomplished.

We worked until about four o'clock that afternoon, by which time we had opened up some fairly large holes in the dam, as well as lowered the top of it to below the existing waterline. By this time, John was working below the middle of the dam, wearing his tall rubber boots in order to keep his feet dry, while I was working on the sides.

"Well, I think we've made a pretty good dent in this thing," said John, standing back to survey our progress. "I'll come back and have another go at it tomorrow and see if I can't open it up fully in one or two spots. That ought to allow enough water to drain out of the marsh to see the trail again."

"So you'll be able to take those wooden stringers out of the trail, right, and people can walk on the path again until it dries up" I asked hopefully.

John wasn't as optimistic on this issue as was I, and he looked at me while shaking his head.

"No, I think that I'd better leave that wood in the trail. Beavers are always making the rounds of their lodges and dams, and they'll notice the water level dropping in a hurry. Believe me, I wouldn't be surprised if they're out here tonight working on fixing the holes while we're asleep!"

I had a long hike ahead of me the next day, as I had already spent a full "unauthorized" day working on the dam. True, it was trail work that had to get done. But our boss Tom Eakin had laid out specific sections of trails to cover on different days, and I was now a full day behind because of this work. Knowing that I had to go from West Lake all the way to Cedar River Flow, then double back to Cedar Lakes again (roughly sixteen miles), I hit the trail early the next morning without stopping by the beaver dam.

The sun had been up for about an hour when I crossed over the wooden boards which led across the flooded marsh flats. Looking down into the water, I noticed that it was still flooded, but it appeared to be about an inch lower than the previous day. Perhaps this was wishful thinking, because I had no way of actually measuring the water depth. But the boards seemed to be a little higher out of the water, and I felt pleased that I had been a factor in that success.

I didn't see John again for about three weeks. My next week's schedule took me down into the Silver Lakes Wilderness area south of Lake Pleasant, which was less familiar territory to me. The following week, John must have been out of the woods for a few days, because his cabin was locked up tight as I made my way up the Placid Trail from Spruce Lake. That was always an ambitious part of my route, with long "legs" on each day. Because of this, I didn't have time to stop by the dam and see the rest of John's work. However, I did notice that the water level had not changed much, and that there was still standing water on the trail.

The next time John and I crossed paths was on the eastern side of Mud Lake. I was heading west from Cedar Lakes in route to a night at Sampson. I saw John ahead of me, steadfastly moving a ladder up against the side of a tar-covered phone pole some distance off the trail.

"Excuse me, Mister Caretaker," I started in, using my best New York City accent. "I'm lost. Can you tell me where the West Canada Lakes caretaker's cabin is? I've heard that he'll cook dinner for you and get your campfire started too!"

John didn't look amused. He was having problems with the ever-problematic squirrel population, and his red face bore testimony to the number of phone poles he'd had to climb that morning.

"Hey, look who's here," he chanted. "Mister Smoky Bear!" Looking at his watch, he decided that he'd had enough for the morning. "What do you say we head back and have something cold to drink? Might replace some of the blood the deerflies sucked out of you!"

I readily agreed to follow John back to his cabin to rest for a spell. John was a very easy person to get along with, once he got to know and trust you. He had become one of my favorite people, and he was one of the primary reasons I had returned to the West Canada Lakes region for a third successive year. I enjoyed his company, and hopefully the feeling was mutual.

As we made our way down the final gentle slope to cross the marsh, I asked John about the dam. After all, it was part of his actual duties to keep the trail cleared, and he had put a lot of time and effort into the task. I had only served as his temporary assistant for the day.

"Have you been over that stretch of trail in the last week?"

146

he asked angrily, a glint in his eye as he turned to face me.

"Well, yes, I went by there sometime last weekend. It didn't look a whole lot better yet, but I didn't know if the water had had a chance to drain." After all, it had rained quite a bit the week before, and the spongy soil tended to feed its wetness into the lakes for several days following a good soaking.

"No, it's not the rain," John replied. "Come on, let's take a detour and I'll let you take a look at our work."

Following along at a brisk pace, I could tell that whatever John was going to show me was not good news. He was obviously perturbed, and I thought I knew what was coming.

Cutting across the west side of the marsh and heading downstream, we arrived at the site of the dam. The one that we had worked so hard to pull apart. The sticks, the limbs, the rocks. All that sweat and all those tools. For what?

I found myself standing next to John, looking at a beautiful new (or should I say reconstructed) beaver dam, about twenty to twenty-five feet across and four feet tall. It was, in essence, the same dam that we had taken apart just a short month ago. It would have been tough to tell whether the beavers had located and reused some of the very material that John had dragged off into the woods. However, there it was, standing strong and firm, efficiently plugging off the stream that led to West Lake.

As I stood there, commiserating with John over the sight of the newly completed work, I noticed something new. The beavers, in their infinite wisdom, had decided to add a few choice pieces of lumber that looked like they had once been part of the helicopter pad. It was tough to say for sure, because they would have had to drag that lumber some distance over land in order to get it to the new dam site. However, somewhere in my mind, something clicked. It told me that those beavers would do just about anything to make fools out of us, including taking our walkway and using it to raise the water level even higher.

Silently, I concluded to myself that this was one battle that we were not going to win. The forces of nature working against us here were simply too numerous and too persistent. And somewhere, from inside a beaver lodge not too far away, I could swear that I heard the sounds of laughter.

A postscript to this story: Long after I had left the woods and John Remias had passed away, the beavers completed their aquatic subjugation of this area. The waters rose to a depth that simply could not be spanned by makeshift crossings, and the state decided not to build a permanent structure. The solution was to build a new and widely rerouted trail that avoids the area entirely and adds about a half mile to the route. Sadly, it bypasses some truly wonderful views of Mud Lake as it passes through the adjacent woodland on higher ground.

Once again, Mother Nature had the final word.

Navigating the Trails (and Between!)

The West Canada Lakes Wilderness area is an odd piece of territory because it is so large in size physically and yet receives so few visitors. For my first two years in the area, I patrolled with a partner, although we rarely saw each other, since we were assigned routes that purposefully kept us as strategically separated as possible to maximize our coverage in case of emergency. However, by my third year in the woods, the state finally arrived at the right conclusion, which was that they simply did not need another ranger to cover that area; it couldn't be justified given the small number of users who passed through. My own journal (which I carried to record contacts with hikers) served as testimony to this fact, and it often went many weeks without a single entry.

To some degree, I don't know whether there would have been any human presence back there at all if it weren't for the Northville-Lake Placid Trail. This was the only trail of its kind in Upstate New York. It cut through the heart of the Adirondack Park on a north-south pathway through some genuine wilderness. Certainly there were a number of local fishermen and hunters who frequented these woods, although they tended to disappear before the Fourth of July and reemerge sometime around September. Those people we saw frequenting the trails during the middle of the summer were overwhelmingly the recreational hikers, and a majority of these folks were going from one end of the Northville-Lake Placid Trail to the other.

The reasons people are drawn to the Placid Trail are many and diverse. As John Remias once told me, "These damned hikers are like a flock of lemmings. Get one of them started and thousands will follow, just because there's a trail there. But drop any of them in a spot more than ten feet off the trail and you'd have to round up half the rangers in the state to find them!"

To a degree, I must admit that I had to agree with him, for I had personally spoken with many visitors who carried not a single topographic map in their pack. Yes, a vast majority of hikers, and certainly those with any experience in the woods, came prepared with maps and compasses, although they may have been unversed in their use. However, some of the other aids people used for navigation were far less helpful. I met one fellow from northern Pennsylvania who was hiking the Placid Trail solo, and his only guide was a poorly copied map that displayed only the path of the trail itself, with no landmarks or topographic information. Additionally, he had failed to scan the top third of the map, which must have been left hanging outside of the photocopying machine as he produced the document. The result was a rather barren sheet of copy paper, without a single usable feature other than the major waypoints between the trailheads.

I'm sure that to some folks this system made sense, as the trail itself must have provided some degree of comfort. The worn (and often eroded) swath of dirt that was carved into the woods was quite wide and hard to miss, even when hiking in nearly complete darkness. It was a virtual highway that, if followed with any degree of care, would lead the hiker to the end of the rainbow in Lake Placid. However, anyone who ever became turned around off the trail could attest to the fact that the West Canada Lakes were a very large area, and trying to find one's way out without a map could be a fruitless task.

Over the years, I had seen and heard of a number of cases when people, lost and unable to retrace their steps, perished in the woods due to exposure or hunger. Some of these accounts were probably "urban legends," but others were in fact well documented, and their stories served as reminders of the consequences of entering the woods unprepared.

The old way of navigating involved merely toting a map (hopefully a New York State topographic map) and a compass. The only problem, as John often mentioned, was that the area was liberally blessed with deposits of iron ore, which could wreak havoc with compass readings. I had personally stood in one spot and watched a compass needle spin motor-like in a circle around the balance pin. At such times, moving just ten feet in any given direction would dramatically alter the reading. I opted to ignore such directions and instead align myself with my map and the sun.

For all the traveling I did in my territory, very little was done off the trails, as I was supposed to be interacting as much as possible with the recreational land users. And since they rarely ever ventured off the trails, there was little or no reason for me to do so. I did occasionally travel the abandoned trails between Whitney Lake and the back of Pillsbury Bay on Cedar Lakes, but that was about the extent of it. These trails had not been maintained by the state for many years, although some of the local fishermen had worked to keep them open for their own personal use. They were still easy to follow, even though most hikers would be unable to locate the spots where they diverged from the well-beaten path.

I must admit that a few of the places I had seen on the maps held some appeal to me, and the only reason I did not visit them (besides my own busy schedule) was the fact that they were small and tough to reach. Perhaps the most famous of these spots was Northrup Lake, which was a well-known fishing destination during the early part of the last century. Northrup could be found by leaving the trail halfway between West and Brooktrout Lakes, then heading into the woods on a southwesterly track. The lake itself was a small body of water that was located, according to John, on the side of a mountain.

"I wouldn't even bother looking for it," John had warned me. "I've missed it myself a couple of times, and there's not a lot left there to see. It was fished out years ago and now is about as barren as my bathtub. Besides, it's in the middle of nowhere."

To some degree, I felt that John was being protective of me, as he doubted (and rightfully so) my ability to navigate beyond the trail. However, I did agree with his assessment that probably no one had visited there in the past fifty years. It was many miles off the nearest trail, through endless swamps, and up creek beds that may have dried and vanished. When you considered the fact that the fish were gone and that there was very little to be seen, it further reduced the reason to pay a visit. Unless, of course, you are one of those people who go simply "because it is there," in which case, please feel free!

Since my days of hiking the trails, a modern wonder known as GPS (Global Positioning System) has further opened the woods the to world of the inexperienced hiker. This device works in conjunction with a system of satellites, which orbit the earth while beaming down a stream of navigational data. These signals are processed into a set of directions, which can then guide the hiker (or driver) to a particular location. From what I've heard, the sophistication of these instruments has become so well developed that they can even tell a person when to turn on a particular street. Amazing!

However, GPS systems were not available until about ten years after I left the woods, and as such did not enter into my life as a wilderness park ranger. I was able to see this technology demonstrated first hand, though, when I later revisited the West Canadas many years after my employment. On that trip, I met up with a young married couple from Toronto. The gentleman had been given the device as a Christmas present by his wife, and he was determined to use it throughout their stay in the woods.

"I read all the directions," said Marty, who had introduced himself and his wife, Chris, an hour earlier. "But for some reason, when I tried getting even a simple reading, I couldn't seem to come up with a thing!"

Chris sat behind her husband and watched intently as he played with the buttons and settings, all the while smiling patiently. She wore an expression that was partially smug, as if to say "I could do that if I wanted to," while still maintaining an air of calm understanding. After all, since she had bought the contraption for him in the first place, she could hardly complain if it was difficult to use or read. She was in a spot.

As Marty continued to wrestle with the keyboard, I commiserated with him over his predicament. I was no longer in uniform, yet I felt the need to help him.

"Did you need to enter a set starting point before you came into the woods?" I inquired. I didn't have a clue whether you needed to do this or not, but it seemed like a logical place to start.

"Yeah, I've taken care of all that," he replied. "And I've put in fresh batteries, and I read all the instructions and everything. But it's been really tough to use. I think that the trees are blocking out a lot of the signals, because I'm not even getting a reading most of the time. It's a good thing that we're not relying on it to make it to Piseco, because we'd be totally lost by now!"

It made me feel better to know that these good people had a back-up system, the tried and true topographical map, to provide directions through to the trailhead in Piseco. However, when I saw the relic that they presented, which was many years old and in horrible condition, I was concerned. I felt the urge to offer them my map, which I certainly didn't need. Instead, I decided to provide verbal directions for any spots that might be confusing and told them to stick to the Northville-Placid trail markers that would walk them along the path to civilization. After all, if I gave a map to everyone who was without one, I'd need to carry a separate rucksack on each excursion into the woods...and I hadn't even been a ranger in over a decade!

For that matter, the maps that I saw while on the job varied greatly in age and condition. For the most part, our hikers carried in versions that were current and fairly up-to-date, since the Adirondack Mountain Club had issued a hiking guide that was specific to the Northville-Lake Placid Trail. (I myself carried a complete series of New York State topographic maps of the region, which were much more comprehensive. I felt that I would need them in the event of a search for a missing person.) But I often saw versions that were either very outdated or extremely worn.

On one occasion, I saw a map that had been separated into a series of small, index card-sized pieces. I had to laugh, as it reminded me of the maps we cut up when creating our own waterproof guides, which were then attached to folded sections of cheesecloth. But in this case, the users were left guessing as to how the pieces fit together. It was interesting to see them attempting to match up the squares of material, turning them upside down and right side up as they tried to form a continuous set of topographic lines.

I knew as I watched them that I had no need to worry. For even as they pieced together their veritable jigsaw puzzle of a map, it was clear that they knew where they were going. Local knowledge counts for a lot in the woods, and while a map is very important (and can be critical), almost anyone can navigate the trail system if they have seen it before and they stick to the trails.

One situation that I encountered during my third year in the woods was quite a bit worse. And to complicate matters even more, I was helpless to do much about it, because on this particular occasion, the duo of hikers I needed to help was unable to speak English.

I had started the morning over at Sampson Lake and hiked through the bright morning sunlight towards West Canada Creek and the junction with the Northville-Lake Placid Trail. Upon my arrival, I followed my normal routine, which was to cross over the bridge to the West Canada Creek lean-to before commencing my trek south to Spruce Lake. It was a very slight diversion, but one that was well worth it. For the price of an extra hundred yards, I could check out the condition of the old lean-to that sat on the banks of the creek and possibly meet a party of hikers who might be camped there.

On this particular morning, I motored quickly along the westerly path from Sampson Lake until I hit the much older Placid Trail. As usual, I was alone throughout this part of my patrol. Sampson Lake was very seldom visited, nor was the pathway that led there from West Lake. I stopped quickly at the lean-to on the creek, which was empty. Since I had already covered about three miles of trail, I felt justified in taking a quick break, removing my pack while sipping some water from my canteen. I also scanned the most recent lines in the lean-to log book, which someone had benevolently placed on the top shelf along the right wall of the shelter. Not many lean-tos had their own log book. Those that did provided some excellent entertainment, as the remarks left by the various hikers, campers, and fishermen were stoked with wit and humor.

In any case, I stayed for about ten minutes before resaddling my pack and commencing the trek south. I would be heading to the southern end of Spruce Lake today, which would be another six miles. I wanted to get there early in the day in order to go over to Balsam Lake for a quick visit.

As I crossed back over West Canada Creek and started my hike, I heard voices in the distance. They were conversational in nature, not loud or emphatic, just two people talking. Yet they were far enough away that I could not understand the words. As they came closer and into view, I got a glimpse of two young men, both in their late twenties or early thirties, both in great shape, carrying high-tech backpacks and gear.

Their conversation continued until they were within clear sight of me, which was a distance of only twenty-five to thirty yards. Still, I could not understand their words, and I slowly came to the realization that they were not speaking English. They acted stunned at seeing anyone there, which I read in their eyes and the way they came to an abrupt halt.

"Hello," I said in a loud voice as we approached each other. "You're up and on the trail rather early this morning. Where are you coming from?"

The point of asking the question was actually moot, as I knew that they were coming up from the south, which meant Spruce Lake. Still, I wanted to talk with them and find out where they started, as well as their destination.

"Hallo! Prego!" was about all that I could get from the hiker in front. The gentleman who followed merely nodded an enthusiastic approval. I could see that this might be a challenge in the making.

"Do you folks speak English?" I asked, all the while flashing my most friendly smile. "Do you need help with anything?"

Even though my smile and slow speech were apparently disarming, neither helped bridge the communications gap with the hikers. From what I could tell, they were Italian and couldn't speak more than a few words of English.

"Way for wateer, eez OK, no?" asked the hiker in front. He smiled again, displaying a set of amazingly white teeth, which contrasted starkly with his wavy dark hair. "Eez OK?"

From what I gathered, the fellow who was in the lead was named Gino. His companion said a few words that seemed to be an introduction, although I must profess ignorance to the pronunciation of his name. It was beyond me. I have always prided myself in my ability to communicate in French, however, Italian, which is also one of the Romance languages, is a mystery to me.

I nodded back at him dumbly as he continued his attempt to establish an understanding.

After about five minutes of playing charades, I finally arrived at the conclusion that they wanted to ask for directions. I derived that by the fact that Gino removed a map from his pack and displayed it briefly in front of my face, all the while asking questions in Italian.

Anyone who has ever tried to speak a language that they did not know can sympathize with my efforts over the next fifteen minutes. I had them follow me back to the creek lean-to, where I unfolded their map onto the front of the lean-to and prepared to give them directions. To what, I did not know, because I couldn't understand the first thing that they were saying. On top of that, I immediately saw that their "map" was nothing more than a diagram drawn onto the back of a folded up paper restaurant placemat! Oh, great! Nothing like a sketch on a placemat from Friendly's to keep you on track!

In any case, I was able to show them, in relative terms, where they were along the way. I also took out my pen and added as many details as I could to their drawing, which was as crude as possible while still bearing some resemblance to the territory. I found it to be about one third useful, one third amusing, and one third scary, all at the same time. In any case, I added drawings of some of the smaller lakes and landmarks, along with tiny sketches of lean-tos at the appropriate places along the trail throug the West Canadas. Then, using my best knowledge of the metric system, I added in distance markers in kilometers, which I prided myself in remembering from years past. They seemed to understand these notations, as they watched over my shoulder and nodded their approval.

Over the course of the next ten minutes, the two Italians proceeded to ask me a string of questions, all in Italian, which prompted repeated shoulder shrugs from me, accompanied by my undoubtedly attractive glassy-eyed stares. At one point, I felt compelled to try giving directions in English with an Italian accent, which I quickly decided was idiotic. No, they would have to figure it out by themselves, or not at all. This one was tough.

After another few minutes of nodding and grinning, all at cues which were entirely non-verbal, we shook hands and parted ways. It was clear to me that they were heading towards Cedar River Flow up on the Moose River Plain and that they were well supplied and experienced. I doubted that there was much else that I could do for them, so I bid them farewell and sent them on their way. When I returned to the woods the following week via Perkins Clearing, I looked for them around Cedar Lakes. However, they had apparently already passed through and were on their way back home (or to Italy, for all I knew). But it ended well, so I let it go at that. Their placemat from Friendly's had done the trick, and that's all that mattered.

Even though the hikers from this international expedition could not speak English and had no genuine map, they at least had a rendition that showed the direction and orientation of the major waypoints along the route. That is one level better than the worst situation I saw, which truly stands out in my mind.

It was on a cold afternoon during the first days of September, just prior to Labor Day. I was preparing to wind down and hike out of the woods for the final time that year. Very few people came through after Labor Day, which was when the state decided we would terminate coverage in the West Canada Lakes. A few of my ranger colleagues were kept on through the first snows up in the High Peaks, but this was the end of the season for us.

As I sat down by the lean-to near the dam on Cedar Lakes, I started up a small fire to boil some water for tea. As I did so, I kept my eye on a pair of figures that appeared on the south end of the dam-bridge. My guess was that they had hiked in from Perkins Clearing, since it was already past noon and they had obviously not come from the Placid Trail. I also guessed that they were local fishermen, as the sportsmen were starting to return in numbers now that the weather was cooling.

Within a few minutes, a gentleman with prematurely gray hair who appeared to be in his mid-forties appeared around the corner of the lean-to. He was accompanied by a youthful boy who was in his teens, whom I assumed to be his son.

"Are you the ranger around here?" he asked in a friendly tone. "We're new to these parts, and I just want to make sure that we're on track."

I agreed to help and asked the father to show me their route on his map. What followed was simply astounding.

"Well, we don't exactly have a map," he said. "We have friends down on Lake Pleasant who invited us up for the week. They told us to follow this route back here. Let me show you where it goes."

With that, he pulled a small piece of material out of a side pocket of his pack and carefully handed it to me. I was dumb-founded. It wasn't a map of any kind. Instead, it was a napkin that contained a short list of locations that read as follows:

- Go from Perkins Clearing into woods
- Follow trail to Cedar Lakes (avoid Pillsbury Lake trail)
- From Cedar Lakes, proceed to Cedar River Flow lean-to
- From Cedar River Flow lean-to, hike to Wakely Dam
- At Wakely Dam, call us from the ranger station. We'll pick you up.

Wow, this was new. No map at all! Simply a napkin with names. No distances, no landmarks, nothing. (But in the event of a spilled cup of coffee, they'd have something with which to clean!)

As I sat there looking at this document, I tried my best to pre-arrange my speech. After all, I felt the need to say something to this fellow, who had just walked close to ten miles into the woods trusting his own safety and that of his son to nothing more than a napkin. And while I hated to lecture a man in front of his son, I felt that this had to be addressed.

159

Yet, as I spent the next ten minutes trying to convince my new friends of the importance of bringing along a map and compass, I had the distinct impression that I was having absolutely no affect at all. Some people were reasonable, logical-minded individuals who could understand the need for such equipment. This fellow did not fit into that category, and I was obviously wasting my time trying to win him over.

"OK," he moaned as I presented my case, "If you really think it's important, perhaps you could draw me a quick map and we'll leave it at that. But I really don't think that it's necessary. The trail is very well marked. Isn't it?"

I agreed that it undoubtedly was, but that it couldn't hurt to carry along a map of the area to show the relative distances and side trails to serve as additional guides. As I pulled out my own map, I looked for a piece of paper to use in order to provide a tracing. They had no paper of their own, and the only thing that I could find in my pack was the pocket-sized note pad which I used to record my contact with the hikers. It was far too small to render a useful drawing, much less a map showing the entire trail to the Wakely dam.

I ended up by using four or five sheets of the note pad paper, with numbers attached to each in order to show the order of progression along the trail. They probably provided very little in the way of guidance, although there wasn't anything else that I could do at that point. It was the only time in my life that I wished that I had another placemat from Friendly's. So with that and a handshake, I bid them farewell and sent them on their way.

—17—

A Fungus Among Us

I've always said that I am a fairly unadventurous person in many ways. A lot of friends and associates might disagree with that statement, because I've also done a lot of things that are considered on the wilder side of "normal." But in general, I'm not a risk taker.

In contrast to my own staid ways, many of the people I met in the woods were genuine thrill seekers. From whitewater rafting and hot air ballooning on the milder side, to rock climbing (without ropes!) and skydiving on the other end of the spectrum, these folks were unique in their pursuit of adventure. Maybe someday, I thought. (But then again, maybe not!)

My lack of desire for this type of activity even extends to my selection of food. I've never been a meat and potato person, preferring fish and similar substitutes. But I've never felt the need to forage for mushrooms, fungi, and other such saprophytes. I've heard all the horror stories about those unfortunate novices who select the wrong species of these delectables and end up getting very sick. No thanks. I'll stick to the mushrooms that are offered to me on the salad bar.

The woods throughout the West Canada Lakes were filled with numerous members of this spectrum of flora, although I never paid any of them more than a passing glance. With all the downed lumber from the heavily wooded forests, and a thick layer of organic "duff" covering the ground, we were bound to have more than our share of mushrooms and fungi. In addition to those that grew out of the decomposing tree branches and limbs, an endless variety of mushrooms just seemed to spring from the ground. They took on an amazing variety of sizes and shapes, although I never bothered to learn the distinguishing characteristics between the various species.

It was on a damp and cool August afternoon when my interest in these saprophytes was raised to a higher level. I had just arrived from Sampson Lake, covered with a misty dew that had been settling for the past two hours. As I removed the pack from my back on the front log of the Cedar Lakes Dam lean-to, I said hello to a trio of middle-aged hikers who had also just arrived. Two men and a woman, they were likewise damp from the light rain and immediately went about the tasks of setting up house in the comfortable lean-to.

They were rugged-looking professional people who, in modern parlance, would probably be classified as "yuppies." But they were very friendly and very well-equipped with the latest in packs and hiking gear. Often, when I met people who were high on the spectrum of experience in the woods, I limited the educational aspect of my conversation to answering their questions or giving directions. These people fit that description.

The most scholarly looking of the three introduced himself to me as Greg, a biology teacher from the Utica school district. In addition to his long locks of salt-and-pepper hair, he had a slightly overgrown beard that had a decidedly silver appearance to it. I could easily picture him evolving into a wizened-looking wizard within the next ten years; he had "academia" written all over him. He quickly introduced his two friends, Martha and Jeff, both of whom had hiked with him before.

"I have the whole summer off to do whatever I want," Greg said as he removed some outer garments from deep in his pack. "So I use a lot of it to go hiking in various parts of the park. But my friends don't have that luxury, so we try to do about a week of hiking each summer. This is it."

"That sounds like a plan," I replied. "Have you been back here before, or is this your first visit?"

"No, this is our first time," explained Greg. "We're trying to do the entire Placid Trail, but we've got to spread it out over the course of three or four summers. We don't hike very fast, and we like to stop whenever we want without feeling pressured."

"Well, that's certainly the smart way to do it," I said. "I've always felt that far too many people rush through here way too fast, trying to cover huge amounts of ground just to say that they've done the whole 134-mile trail. But what's the use of hiking it if you can't tell people what you've seen when you're done?"

In the background, Martha started to laugh. "Yes, that's exactly the way that we feel. Why rush it? Plus, we don't bother hiking those stretches of trail that follow along the roads. That doesn't make sense either."

Once again, I had to agree with these folks. The first full day of hiking the Northville-Lake Placid Trail, if starting from the very beginning, will send the trekker strolling over several miles of blacktop along Route 30 in Northville and then up several additional miles of smaller paved roads until the trail enters the woods in Upper Benson. Somehow, hiking that stretch never made much sense to me. Other parts of the trail include similar walks over paved and unpaved roads and can be skipped without missing much in the way of a wilderness experience.

I was beginning to feel as though I had a lot in common with these folks, who were far different than many of the younger hikers I met on a daily basis. Well-educated, quiet, and eager to drink in the natural beauty of the setting, they represented my ideal stereotype of what the well-behaved hiker should be.

Until they started eating the campsite.

Well, OK, not exactly the campsite per se. Just some of the living parts of it. For as I stood there listening to their conversation, Jeff stooped down to the ground, plucked a small brown mushroom from near the well-used tent site, and popped it into his mouth. The move surprised me so much that I know my jaw was positively hanging on the ground.

Jeff seemed perfectly aware that I was watching him, for he chuckled as he munched, relishing the taste of the small bit of food.

"Well, if you're just going to leave them around here to spoil, I'm going to have myself a snack," he said with a grin. Both Greg and Martha seemed to nod their approval, and I continued to watch in awe as he finished consuming his hors d'oeuvre, smacking his lips in delight. Wow!

"You know," I said after taking a moment to recover, "I've lived back here for almost two years now, and I've never seen anyone do that. I wouldn't even know how to recognize the good mushrooms from the bad mushrooms myself. How do you do it?"

"Oh, it's really quite simple," Jeff replied, nodding his head over at Greg. "He's the one who got me started on it. There are a few bad ones that you've got to look out for, but most of them are just fine for consuming. And they're really quite flavorful, once you acquire the taste for them."

I had no doubt that they would be, if you could tell with one hundred percent certainty the good from the bad. But I had read all too many stories of novice mushroom pickers who had become violently ill from eating the wrong species, often with long-lasting consequences. (Unfortunately, some of these "bad" varieties bear a striking resemblance to those which are perfectly OK.) I had long ago decided to stay away from this type of activity.

As the afternoon progressed, the three hikers went about their tasks, getting ready for the evening meal, while I backtracked up the lake to check on the Beaver Pond lean-to. I had developed the habit of making my rounds in the late afternoon, as most of our campers would have arrived by that hour and would be available for conversation. However, on this particular afternoon I found the lean-to empty, with the exception of the barn swallows, which swooped through the clearing before settling with a flutter into their nest on the top log of the structure. I always enjoyed watching them fly about the site, listening to their rapid melodic call which sounded (to me) like someone screeching, "check it out, check it out, check it out!"

After sitting in the empty lean-to for a few peaceful moments, I started my short stroll back towards the dam, where I knew that my compatriots would be fixing their supper. I also knew that they'd be out collecting firewood for the evening blaze, as that was a part of the woods experience that few groups missed. One of the nice things about sharing a lean-to with other hikers is that I seldom had to do much in the way of wood collecting. Most folks just assumed that I would be busy with my official duties, and so took that task upon themselves.

As I made my way back to the lean-to, I noticed that the mist had stopped, although the sky remained blanketed in a thick layer of gray clouds. I could tell by the weather that it would be a bad night for fishing. The trout by the dam seemed to be most accessible when the sky was open and the water turned calm, which usually happened in the final hour before sunset. At times such as those I could catch myself a fine brook trout dinner with a few casts of the line. But tonight the lake was choppy and the sun was nowhere to be seen. It would be a freeze-dried dinner for certain.

When I rounded the corner of the lean-to and peeked inside, I was surprised to find only Martha there. She was busy getting ready for dinner, peeling carrots and onions, measuring spices and cups of rice into various receptacles. This was a bit unusual, because the majority of our visitors consumed meals that were mostly prepackaged. But never mind, it certainly looked good. In front of the lean-to was a fine stack of carefully broken firewood that had obviously been gathered while I was gone. They must have been hard at work, because the pile looked substantial enough to keep a blaze burning for quite a while.

"Wow, are those two guys bringing down more wood?" I asked. "You certainly are well-prepared; you could have a fire going for most the night with what they've collected already."

Martha looked up from her cooking chores and answered with a smile. "Oh, no, those two are out hunting again. They're at it constantly. No mushroom in the woods is safe with them in the area!" As she spoke, her blue eyes laughed out from under her straight locks of dark blond hair. She looked as though she had resigned herself to the cooking in order to allow Jeff and Greg to pursue that challenge.

As I broke out my own food pack, the two men returned from the hill that borders the lake, obviously satisfied with the results of their hunt. Greg placed a medium-sized stuff sack on the front of the lean-to, from which he extracted about a dozen or so various mushrooms and fungi. It was quite a collection, although I didn't know if this offering would constitute their main course.

Evidently, Jeff knew less about these organisms than did Greg, who had taught him about the subject in the first place. As Greg picked up one saprophyte after another and examined it, he kept up a running banter, describing its species, its flavor and degree of ripeness, and comparing it to others that he had collected in the past. I didn't know that there was so much to the subject, and I listened enthralled. He was quite the expert.

At one point, he picked up a medium-sized brown mushroom that had a orange-like tinge to it. He turned it over in his hands with a thoughtful expression on his face. Finally, after a minute of two of inspection, he said "Mmm, no, I don't think so," and he tossed the discarded item into the tall grass nearby.

Oh, great! What was that supposed to mean? If Jeff had

picked a mushroom that might have been bad, how reliable would the rest of his selections be? I shuddered to think of it, and I quickly conjured up images of having to carry three sickly hikers out of the woods. I sure hoped they knew what they were doing.

Within the next hour, all of the remaining crop was consumed. All of it. Some of the smaller mushrooms were added to the rice and vegetable dish, while a few others were sliced into a pan and fried. The remaining pickings were simply passed around and eaten whole. Ugh!

If I was amused at their eating habits, they were similarly entertained by mine. Instead of preparing my nightly bowl of "DEC stew" (which could contain some pretty interesting ingredients itself), I opted for a meal of freeze-dried chili mac. It was quick and easy: just add three cups of boiling water to the pouch, stir, and then wait for five or ten minutes. Presto... chili mac! I also chose to add a few slices of my trusty rye bread, which lasted inside my pack for weeks at a time.

"I don't see how you can eat that stuff" said Greg, looking up at me as I began slurping my meal. "It's been frozen, freeze dried, heat processed, and then vacuum packed. If there ever was a nutrient in any of that, it's been sucked out ages ago. You're eating a bowl full of nothing."

In a way, I had to agree with him. Although the stuff tasted pretty good when consumed in the woods, it paled a bit if eaten anywhere near civilization. To this day, I'm convinced that everything tastes better when eaten in the back country.

"Yes, I suppose you're right," I replied. "Maybe that's why I have such a hard time keeping weight on in the summer. But I'm back here for so long that it's impossible to carry around real food for the entire stretch. My pack would weigh more than me!"

As they sat there relishing their meal, they eyed my own repast suspiciously. They were even less impressed when I broke out my dessert, which consisted of freeze-dried ice cream. This item had, at the time, newly emerged onto the scene, and it was still laughed at in many of the camping supply stores. The packets were small and light, filled with little round pellets of a Styrofoam-like material that tasted vaguely like ice cream. It came in two flavors, chocolate and vanilla. I've got to admit that I was not completely won over by these "taste treats," but I wanted to see the reaction they would get from my crew of mushroom pickers.

It was exactly what I expected.

Greg was the first to accept a sample, gingerly pushing a vanilla-flavored pellet past his lips. Fascinating, I thought! That would be the exact expression I'd bear if forced to eat one of their mushrooms! Martha also volunteered to give me a review, sampling another chunk while seemingly holding her breath.

Neither of them cared much for my offering. "Tastes like one of those packing pellets you use when you send something through the mail," said Martha, obviously unimpressed. As she spoke, Greg tried to unobtrusively get rid of the rest of his piece into a crumpled bandana. So much for my taste test.

We enjoyed a very nice evening of conversation around the campfire. The skies overhead cleared enough to permit an occasional peek at the stars, and the breeze kept the nighttime bugs at bay. It was a perfect night for sitting by the fire and trading stories.

As I sat there gazing into the flames, I noticed that Jeff slipped a pot of water onto the grate. "Care to join us for a cup of tea?" he asked. It seemed to be part of their nightly ritual, and as I also enjoyed sipping on a good brewed cup, I quickly agreed. Unfortunately, their definition of tea did not agree with mine; I soon discovered that their variety consisted of more of the plant life that they had collected and dried over the past few days of hiking.

Martha pulled a plastic bag of vegetation from her pack and crushed several twigs, leaves, and other assorted vegetative matters into a tea brewing strainer. This was then added to the pot, where it sat for a period of time until the water came to a boil. At that point, I thought it might be rude for me to pull out my box of Lipton orange pekoe tea bags, so I decided to go along for a taste.

Once again, Greg went on the offensive about the commercial varieties of tea. "I don't see why people bother with that stuff you get from the stores. It starts out OK, but they process it to the point where you can't even recognize it. Give me the homemade brew any day of the week. I think you'll like this; I even brought some of my own blackberry brambles from home to get it started."

I do believe that it tasted good...to someone who was used to that sort of thing. To me, it tasted like a pot of hot water. Maybe they used too much water trying to make too much tea. I sipped from my cup until it was gone, as I had nothing against the taste of hot water. However, I politely declined a refill, then made preparations to crawl into my sleeping bag.

The following morning, the three of them prepared to hit the trail moving westward. They had a rather unusual itinerary planned. Rather than going straight through the West Canadas and heading south towards Spruce Lake, they had decided to continue westward a few extra miles and make camp on Brooktrout Lake. There was no doubt that Brooktrout was a beautiful lake with an outstanding lean-to. It had once been legendary fishing waters (thus the name), and the lean-to was perfectly suited for cooler weather. This was due to a massive boulder in front of it, which was at least as tall as the lean-to itself and served to reflect the heat of the campfire back into the shelter. However, as nice a spot as it was, most folks hiking the Northville-Placid Trail were not interested in diverting several miles off the path. This was the sign of people who were more interested in the scenery than in the accomplishment of "doing the trail." I was impressed.

Greg and Jeff approached me before we parted ways that morning. "Hey, any chance we'll catch up with you at South

Lake?" Greg asked. "We'll be there the day after tomorrow. Stop by if you're in the area, and we'll fix you up some dandelion and artichoke salad!"

"Well gee, how could I resist that offer?" I replied. "I'll bring along the croutons and blue cheese and we'll make a meal of it!" I said that in jest, although I think that he had made his offer earnestly. I'm just not sure that I was ready for a follow-up to the mushroom feast and the twig-and-leaf tea.

My own plan for the day was to patrol the path up to the lean-to on Cedar River Flow, then return to Cedar Lakes. It would be a rather monotonous day, since it was not one of my favorite routes. However, it did permit me to hike without my full pack, which I would stash in the woods until I returned later in the day.

My day was fairly uneventful, as was the following evening. The only excitement was provided by meeting a solo woman who was hiking the entire trail in a two week marathon. A resident of Alaska, she selected the Adirondacks because of "the relatively small size of the park."

"Oh yes, I'm sure that you consider it to be large," she said with a smile. "But where I come from, this is a pretty tiny piece of real estate."

It was an unusual perspective, since most of our visitors were overwhelmed with the size and relative desolation of our woods. This was quite rare indeed!

By the time I commenced my hike towards the interior station on West Lake, it was nearly midday on Sunday. The "crowds," which in our area consisted of three or four hiking groups, had already come and gone, and I had watched them pass by in lazy contentment. After all, it was Sunday, the day of rest, right?

It was a warm day for late August, when the temperatures could sink into the 30s by early morning. But the midday sun was getting quite warm, and I was generating a lot of heat as I made my way past Cat Lake and King's Pond in route to West Lake. Cold weather was coming, but it was nowhere to be seen on this day.

By the time I reached the clearing in back of John's cabin on West Lake, I was quite hot. I unsaddled my pack on the stone front porch of the cabin and knocked on the door. John let me in with his usual friendly greeting.

"Well, if it isn't Ranger Larry, coming along to watch the hikers!" he chortled. John was always amused at the way I tried to keep track of the traffic flow through the territory, even though it was the sole reason for my presence on the state payroll. "You issued any traffic tickets this week?"

"Not yet. At least none that I remember," I replied. "You have much in the way of campers this weekend?"

"For cryin' out loud, they're all over the place!" John said, his voice matching the sour expression on his face. "I can't hardly walk out the door without tripping over someone," he added.

"You wouldn't believe some of the stuff that's been going on around here today," John continued. "We had some of them nature-food berry-pickers walking around the clearing, picking up mushrooms and all kinds of odds 'n ends. They're out of their cotton-pickin' minds, I tell you!"

I had to laugh at that one. "Yes, John, I know exactly who you're talking about. I met them down at Cedars two days ago. They're still here; I saw their name in the register book when I passed through the backyard. They're nice enough people, but they ate every mushroom within three hundred yards of the lean-to!"

John was not similarly impressed, as he had his own views on this type of behavior. "Well, I tried talking to this guy, but he seemed to know it all already," he said. "He was walking around picking mushrooms in the mud patch over by the edge of the clearing. I tried telling him that he might not want to pick there, but he insisted on doing it anyway."

I had to laugh at that one. "You mean, over where the old outhouse used to be?" I asked. The rickety old structure had stood there for many years, despite the fact that John's main outhouse was on the other side of his clearing. It had finally become unsafe for use, as the wood was rotting through and the unwary user stood the very real chance of falling through the plank flooring.

"Yup, that's the spot!" replied John. "His eyes were glued to the ground...didn't seem to want to talk to me in the least. So finally, I just said 'The heck with it, go ahead and eat 'em if you want!'"

I threw back my head and gave myself up to laughter. Of course, it was no wonder the soil there would have been a prime growing spot. Just look at all the fertilizer that had been deposited there over the years!

"I tell you, Larry," he continued. "I don't know why I bother trying to talk to these people at all. They're all so smart that they don't need me. That part's obvious."

"Oh, come on, John, just because they're a bit different than you doesn't mean that you shouldn't talk to them," I countered.

"Talk to THEM?" he shouted. "They wanted nothing to do with me. They just wanted me to get out of their way so they could do as they damn well pleased. Heck, maybe I shouldn't have cut the grass this week so they could have grazed on the stuff!"

John had a point there, and there wasn't much else that I could say. I knew for a fact that John had experienced problems with hikers coming through and "borrowing" the tomatoes that he grew in the vegetable patch out back. And while John never had any intentions of utilizing the mushrooms that grew about his cabin, he nevertheless couldn't accept the fact that others would do so without first consulting him. It was a simple case of John being John. I decided not to intervene on behalf of either party, since I enjoyed the company of both.

Later on that evening, I stopped into the West Lake #1 lean-to, located just south of John's cabin. There, I found George, Jeff, and Martha, comfortably finishing up another dinner of mushroom stew and rice. They had hiked the relatively short distance from Brooktrout Lake during the afternoon and would be heading south towards Spruce Lake in the morning.

It was a fitting ending to the episode, although I had already set up my tent in another location and would not be repeating the nightly routine with this group. As pleasurable as our stay together had been, they were campers and I was the ranger. It was time to move on.

However, as I headed back towards my campsite, which was located in a bit of woods hidden from view and well off the trail, I decided that perhaps they had found something that I had overlooked. Maybe they had discovered a part of life in the backwoods that was, indeed, more "woodsy" than I could ever be. After all, they were foraging for their food, whereas I, when prevented from fishing, was relegated to eating unidentifiable bits of freeze-dried comestibles from a pouch. Maybe *I* was the one who needed to learn from *them*.

These thoughts weighed heavily on my mind as I stoked my camp stove and lit the gas-fed flame, (I used this stove often when I camped at a site without a fireplace, for fear of starting a ground fire.) but I realized that I would sooner attempt to do brain surgery than pick out the lethal versus non-lethal varieties of mushrooms that bloomed in my territory.

As I pondered these points, I fished around within the depths of my food pack, looking for something that was not quite so processed as my other meals. Something that would allow me to feel more connected with my surroundings. Something just a little more natural.

I continued looking until my eyes struck pay dirt. There, at the very bottom of the pack, was the answer to my search. It represented the perfect compromise between their world and mine, and I felt a strong desire to sprint over the hill to their lean-to in order to gain their approval. However, I managed to maintain my composure and remain in place.

I set the cook pot to boil while preparing my feast. It would be a very simple affair: open the pouch and add three cups of boiling water. Then stir, and wait five to ten minutes. It was all so easy.

With something akin to awe, I followed the rudimentary instructions, sniffing the aromatic steam as it arose from the pouch. It was like magic. One moment, it was water plus food pouch. The next, it was a gourmet meal for one. Who could ask for more?

When finally it came time to devour the contents, I dove in, taste buds first. I was in heaven, and I rapidly consumed the entire entrée. It was magnificent, even though it was processed and packaged with preservatives added rather that found in nature that way. But that was OK, because I gained a certain amount of self-respect looking down at the empty wrapper, which was now turning brown in the heat of the fire. It read, in bold letters, "Beef Burgundy, with rice *and wild mushrooms*."

Somewhere, somehow, I'm sure that George, Jeff, and Martha would have been proud.

—18—

Random Thoughts on the Woods

Living and working deep inside one of the most desolate parts of the Adirondack Park gave me a unique outlook its current use and future development. I got to interface with people on both sides of "the debate"—those who wanted to develop the Park and its lands as well as those who were opposed to any development at all. It was a topic that could serve as the catalyst for loud and passionate confrontations, because people tend to have very strong feelings on the fate of the Adirondacks depending on where they live and work.

Before working as a wilderness park ranger, I tended to see only one side of the issue. I was all for including as much of the Park in the designated wilderness area as possible, with no option for development. All motorized vehicles were bad, and we should bring back all of the original predators, including mountain lions, sabertooth tigers, and Bigfoot.

It didn't take me long to discover that there are two sides to all of these issues, and that the local population was often the "odd man out" when it came to restricting land use. John Remias put it succinctly when he said that "There's enough wilderness here for everyone." Yet that fact is often forgotten as we go about the business of drawing demarcation lines inside the Park to decide what can be done where.

Prior to the enforcement of the restrictions placed upon designated wilderness regions, motorized vehicles were permitted into and out of most of the territory where I worked. That didn't mean much, as you couldn't drive a vehicle back into any of those places with the possible exception of Pillsbury Lake and the outer reaches of Whitney Lake. But float planes, such as those operated by the Bird family or Herb Helms, could land on most of the lakes back there, including Cedar and West Lakes, often bringing in groups of older campers who otherwise couldn't have made the trip. This entire segment of the population, many of whom were locals who had been back there for most of their lives, were effectively barred from using the woods once those restrictions were put in place.

During my tenure in the West Canada Lakes from 1979-1981, there was still one lake where the floatplanes could land. That was Whitney Lake, which was a smaller body of water near the trail that went from Pillsbury Lake to Sampson Lake. It's a safe bet to say that most non-local hikers who strayed down that route would walk by it without knowing that it was there.

Personally, I never minded the floatplanes landing on Whitney. It was an irregular occurrence throughout the summer; once every few weeks, you'd hear a small-engine plane reducing in altitude, the sound becoming a little louder before disappearing entirely as it dropped onto the water. Then, within a half hour, you'd hear it revving its engine to take off, and then it was gone. No big deal. I just couldn't imagine how that would ruin anyone's wilderness experience.

A number of events have served to change the way the lakes and lands are accessed in the West Canada Lakes region, many of which are due to the land swap between New York State and International Paper, the largest private land owner in the region.

The logging road out of Perkins Clearing, once closed off to all public travel, is now completely accessible for anyone who wants to make the six mile drive off Route 30. The first two miles beyond Perkins Clearing is easily driven in almost any kind of vehicle, including passenger cars that were never meant to be taken "off-road." From that point, you can either turn to the right and drive through Sled Harbor, or you can stay on the logging road toward the new trailhead for Spruce Lake, which is an option that I never had while I was working for the state.

The road up the hill past Sled Harbor is a very rough route and should only be attempted by high-clearance four-wheel drive trucks. I tried to maneuver my passenger car up that hill several years ago, and I regretted it almost immediately. I could hear the scraping sounds as the boulders in the road tore at the exposed bottom of my exhaust system. To this day, I wonder how many dollars-per-mile I paid in repairs as a result of that trip.

I have been back into Cedar Lakes twice now since the hike in was shortened from eight miles to about five (assuming you have a four-wheel drive vehicle) when they put a parking lot at the bottom of the Pillsbury Mountain trail. I was curious to see how this would impact the use (or abuse) of Cedar Lakes, Pillsbury Lake, and other nearby waterways. I was pleased to see that neither of these lakes seemed to be suffering any visible consequences from the increased accessibility, and the usage (as measured by people signing the register) appeared to be relatively unchanged.

An even more radical change is the logging road that now approaches Spruce Lake, providing a trailhead that is perhaps only a few miles from the lake itself. For most of the time I was working the trails of the region, Spruce Lake required a long, tough eleven miles of drudgery, on wet trails that seemed to go up and down over every topographic line in the territory. It was one of the tougher routes into the West Canada Lakes. Then during my last year, I was startled to see the logging road being widened nearby the Jessup River, within a few short miles of the southern end of the lake. It seemed to appear out of nowhere. Suddenly, Spruce Lake just didn't seem as wild as it once had, and the door into the heart of the West Canadas themselves had been thrown wide open.

I must admit that I regretted these changes, as I liked the fact that it required several days to reach the interior of our woods. There was something about the remoteness, the very "distantness" of West Lake that appealed to me, although it was always possible to hike in from the Moose River Plains via Brooktrout Lake in a single day.

Our territory has also changed over time due to the disappearance of many of the trail systems. At one time, an entire network of footpaths encircled the West Canada Lakes region, with trails extending to what are now less-frequented bodies of water such as Twin Lakes, Northrup Lake, and Otter Lake.[4] Trails also entered the territory from the west, providing access to streams and ponds that are unused today. It is hard to believe that any of these places have been visited by more than a dozen people in the past fifty years.

The disappearance of so many trails is actually not a matter of conservation. Rather, it is the lack of funding that has restricted the ability of the DEC to hire crews to clear and maintain the footpaths through the region. A tree that falls across the trail today may go uncleared for a period of years, forcing people to create diversionary routes into the woods around them. It has often crossed my mind that the very existence of the Northville-Lake Placid Trail could be placed in peril should the Adirondacks ever receive a violent storm that knocks down thousands of trees in its path.

During my last visit, which was in the summer of 2007, I found

[4] The USGS topographic maps of 1903 and 1954 show numerous trails that have been gone for over fifty years. The earlier of these also shows a road that entered the region from the West and followed the course of West Canada Creek up to its origin at the outlet of Mud Lake. However, this road was already gone from the 1954 map.

that the southern spur trail that left the NLP Trail for Sampson Lake was now completely gone. However, the trail that departs for Sampson from West Canada Creek still exists, although it is badly overgrown.

The other trail that seems to have disappeared is the Otter Brook Trail from the Moose River Plains. It enters the region from the north and intersects the NLP Trail at a point just east of Beaver Pond on Cedar Lakes. While still on the topographic maps, it appears completely abandoned and is probably very tough to follow except where there are a few remaining trail marker signs. Even in the late 1970s, this access route was seldom used (I only met one group who came into Cedar Lakes on it) and was never a major thoroughfare.

The absence of the trail crews today has caused problems, even with the major routes such as the NLP Trail. In a number of areas, trees and brush along the sides of the trails are so overgrown that they actually come together in the middle, leaving hikers to push their way through the dense vegetation. The weeds and undergrowth in the clearing that used to surround the West Lake Canada Lake caretaker's cabin are so overgrown that they are starting to hide the trail signs, leaving hikers to guess which direction to proceed.

In other places, the water level has risen due to beaver activity, and hikers have constructed crude walkways out of materials salvaged from earlier bridges and structures. It is a crude and makeshift way around the budget cut predicament, but it has worked so far. And, as John Remias was fond of saying, "Hikers shouldn't be afraid of getting their feet wet while walking through the wilderness."

In lieu of the state-sponsored trail crews, the Adirondack Mountain Club has stepped in and taken over some of this work on a voluntary basis. Almost all of their chapters have "adopted" stretches of trail, which they repair and groom while spending extended weekends in the woods. In the case of the West Canada

Lakes region, the Genesee Chapter of Rochester, New York, has adopted the Sucker (Colvin) Brook trail, which runs from Lewey Lake Campground to its intersection with the NLP Trail north of Cedar Lake. Their work has been invaluable in keeping that trail open and in shape for public use.

Over the years, the course of the trails through the West Canada Lakes Wilderness Area have changed dramatically. This point is highlighted when you compare the various versions of the USGS topographic maps from over the years. The NLP Trail had not yet been built as of the time the 1954 edition was printed. However, many trails that did appear on that year's map were already gone without a trace by the time I arrived in 1979.

It has been a constantly evolving scene, although it's probably safe to say that the days of new trail construction are over. Through it all, the West Canada Lakes region has managed to avoid its share of the hiker traffic that has overwhelmed many of the other wilderness tracts in the state. It is this fact, coupled with the great work of a few dedicated volunteers, which has kept these woods in the pristine condition that we have come to know and love. I can only hope that this can be maintained into the future so that our children and grandchildren can make the same statement when we are gone.

—19—

The Indian Dinner

"Everything tastes better in the woods."

That is a statement that I know, for a fact, is true. I have seen some highly questionable concoctions prepared with the worst looking ingredients, yet in the woods it all seems to taste pretty darn good. My own theory is that you get a lot hungrier than you think while stomping around the trails, performing demanding tasks that burn up mountains of energy. By the time the dinner bell rings in camp, most of us really don't care what's in the pot. Shoe leather with gravy would probably fit the bill just fine! (Remember to pack a sharp knife.)

Over the years, I have had only a couple genuine failures that could not be recovered. These were my one attempt at matzo ball soup and a freeze-dried cheese fondue that bore a striking resemblance to bookbinder paste. But other than those two, it was all pretty good. Some of my meals tasted better than others, mind you, and I tended to prefer my own version of "DEC Stew" over some of the sterile looking freeze-dried meals, but they were all quite tasty when eaten in the woods.

The trouble arose, however, after I had completed my first

couple years on the job and started getting bored with the same old meals every week. That was back in the old days, when there were perhaps a half-dozen dinners in a rather limited portfolio of freeze-dried pouches. Some were distinct in flavor, such as the franks and beans or the chili, and I usually carried along at least one of those each week. Others weren't, despite the variety of chicken dishes I tried, all of which attempted to camouflage the same old bird in a plethora of sauces, they all tasted pretty much the same. I needed a change.

My experimentation started out using some pretty un-woodsy material. As I've mentioned in other places, I grew rather fond of a major brand of canned Chinese sweet-and-sour chicken, which I'd pour over a package of crispy Chinese noodles. Since this all came in a can, I always ate that meal on my first night in the woods, as I had no desire to carry around a pack of full cans throughout the week. However, it was a real treat, and I looked forward to it every Friday. Then, I'd simply burn out the empty can and carry out the crushed remains. It worked.

But I still longed for variety, so I kept looking for even more possibilities. My partner on the trails the first year, John Wood, had found a company that produced a completely cooked and ready-to-eat dinner, sealed in foil, that contained meat, vegetables, and sauce. But it was very expensive, and the portion size looked too small to satisfy me with a single serving, so I passed on that idea.

I spent quite a bit of time hunting between the camping stores and the other specialty food shops without much success. I was about to give up hope until I happened to come upon an interesting possibility while shopping in the local grocery store in South Glens Falls on one of my days off. It was hidden amongst the dried rice packages in the international food section, which included samplings from a number of continents and countries.

"Indian Dinner," the box proclaimed in bold red letters. It was an open invitation to me, because I have always enjoyed

Indian food. Whether it is a mildly blended biryani or a fiery hot curry, I love it all. So I was pleased as punch to see that this dish contained everything in one easy-to-fix meal. The rice, the meat, the veggies—they were all just sitting in there, waiting to be rehydrated to their native state. The description on the box went on to tell of the lovely spices that were carefully blended together to form this masterpiece of culinary delight. I was positively hooked before I even read the cooking directions. I wanted to take this into the woods, AND SOON!

I placed three boxes of my newly discovered treasure gently into my shopping cart and proceeded through the checkout line. Since it was Wednesday afternoon, I still had another day and a half before heading back into the woods. Because of this, I thought it might be a good idea to try one of these Indian dinners ahead of time, just to see whether I liked it or not. I really couldn't see not enjoying "the blended spices of India," but I also didn't want to end up in the woods with a meal I didn't like.

At that time, I was staying in Glens Falls with my then-girlfriend, Patty. In those days, she was working in the Glens Falls Hospital as a medical technologist. On that particular evening, she had been assigned the second shift duty, meaning that she had to work from three until eleven o'clock. This wasn't a problem, but it did mean that we wouldn't be having dinner together that evening. Instead, she would eat an early meal before going to work, and then have a bit more to eat while on break later in her shift. I was left to fend for myself and prepare my own dinner. Perfect! Indian Dinner to the rescue!

Patty lived in a very old building in the middle of downtown Glens Falls. It is right across the street from where they have since built the sports arena, which revitalized the heart of the city. The bottom floor was a very nice store, which was occupied by the owner of the building. But the upstairs two floors were a bit run down and hadn't been used in many years. That was until the owner decided to pump a lot of money into renovations, which he used to convert the second floor into office space and the third floor into a pair of luxurious apartments. They were big, spacious, and modern, with fresh carpeting and paint gracing the surfaces. Everything was new, including the kitchens and bathrooms, which sat gleaming below expanses of twelve-foot ceilings. It was impressive.

Unfortunately for the owner, the other tenant had decided to move out that week on very short notice. He was left scrambling to try to find a new tenant, which is not always easy to do in the middle of a busy work schedule. Since he was making a few last-minute upgrades to the other apartment, he had asked Patty whether it was OK if he brought his prospects through her apartment. She agreed, and the time was established for the tour.

"OK, now don't forget," Patty said to me, as she got her things together for work, "They'll be coming through tonight around seven o'clock. So try to keep the place looking neat, and leave all the doors to the rooms open."

I agreed to do so, as I knew it was important that the landlord rent out the other apartment as soon as possible so that he wouldn't have to increase Patty's rent. He needed to make a good showing, and I wanted to help.

In order to increase the overall appeal of the place, I went out into the hallway and moved my hiking boots and socks from view. They were quite muddy, and, on top of that, my socks were always wet and odorous by the time I left the woods each week. This day was no exception; they stunk. (I wouldn't have been surprised to see them get up and walk in the door by themselves!) I gingerly lifted them between my thumb and forefinger and placed them into a zip-locked bag, which I sealed and hid inside a closet. Things looked better already.

By the time I had cleaned up the hallway and further straightened up inside, it was after five-thirty, and I was getting hungry. I hadn't been hiking up a monstrous appetite as I did in my normal environment, but I also hadn't eaten much that day, so I was ready for a good dinner.

I got out the box of Indian Dinner and began boiling the water in a small pot on the stovetop. I don't believe the apartment had a microwave oven, as they hadn't yet become as popular as in later years, so I was forced into the slow cooking method. No problem, as that would allow the spices to bubble together and better mix with the rest of the ingredients.

The meal cooked as advertised, and I extended the process by lowering the heat and allowing the meat and rice to slowly soak up all the juices. There were also plenty of beans mixed in with the other ingredients, and the total scent was wonderful. Big, billowing clouds of aromatic steam wafted out of the pot, sending the smell of Indian food across the kitchen and down the hall. I was drooling in anticipation by the time I removed the vessel from the stove.

OK, it was now showtime, and I was ready for a feast. I still had close to an hour before the apartment tour was supposed to begin, which meant that I'd be able to genuinely savor my meal. As I sampled that first forkful of curry, my eyes closed in reverence. It was everything I had dreamed of and more. Those spices came through in an avalanche of flavor, exploding in my mouth. As a matter of fact, it was even stronger than I had expected. Much stronger. The taste of curry was very, very powerful, and I found myself quickly reaching for the water pitcher. The dark yellow coloration of the serving bowl bore testimony to the heavy doses of tumeric, cumin, and coriander that must have been mixed into the dish. Wow! This was really something.

As I chewed my meal, I tried to picture just how this would taste on the shore of Cedar Lakes. The scent would no doubt attract the attention of the local bear population. Of that I had no doubt; it was that strong. But not to worry; I hadn't hung food once in three years, as there had never been a bear that caused a problem. It just wasn't an issue back there as it was in the High Peaks.

I was daydreaming away, considering a number of these

thoughts as I polished off the entire bowlful of Indian Dinner. It was supposedly a portion for two people, but I demolished it within a relatively short period of time. I decided that it would be a great addition to my backpack, and that I would proudly carry it into the West Canada Lakes that following week. I'd be the envy of the local hiking population. (That is, if anyone was back there.)

I quickly cleaned the dishes and put the kitchen in order, finishing by around six forty-five. Ah yes, right on schedule. I still had about fifteen minutes before the tour was to begin. With nothing else to occupy my time, I walked into the living room and turned on the television, hoping to catch the end of the nightly newscast. This was something that I liked to do on occasion, as it let me relax while catching up on the events of the week.

The television flickered on as I put my feet up on the couch, pleasantly feeling the edge of drowsiness creeping up on me. This was a real luxury, and I felt as though I could doze off at any time. I was completely comfortable with the world.

Well, maybe not.

As I lay there digesting my dinner, I heard a series of loud bubblings and gurglings coming from inside my body. Most distinctly, they were issuing from my gut, and they were growing in volume. Even worse, I detected a bloated feeling that started out mild, but increased in intensity within the first minute or so. It didn't feel good.

Over the next few minutes, I experienced what can only be described as a "rapid inflation of the body cavity," which was accompanied by an increasing need to rid myself of the causal gas. I tried to avoid doing so, as I was expecting the landlord to show up at any minute with his prospect, ready to show off the premises. However, after attempting to contain myself for a period of about three minutes, I detonated, which resulted in a high pitched musical note that was (I believe) a C sharp.

The resulting odor that surged forth into the apartment was

beyond description. It was a cross between many things, including Indian Dinner and methane gas. It was tremendously powerful, horrible, and capable of penetrating solid walls of granite. And worse yet, I felt myself refilling with fumes at an ever increasing rate of speed.

Indian Dinner. What the hell was going on?

I couldn't leave the apartment, as the landlord was relying on me to let him in for the tour. So I dashed as quickly as possible into the bathroom and turned on the fan, hoping to vent the fumes into the outside atmosphere. It didn't work. To make matters worse, my body was now in "continuous vent" mode, never more than twenty to thirty seconds away from the next expulsion. It was serious. I thought I was going to explode into a million little pieces of myself.

As I stood in the bathroom behind the closed door, with the fan going full tilt, I thought to myself, "OK, what the heck do I do now?" I never had the chance to answer that question. The apartment doorbell did it for me.

I opened the door to the bathroom, allowing another wave of toxic waste fumes to surge into the hallway. I felt as though it carried me down the hall to the door, alleviating the need to walk. It was about as bad as it could get, and it was distributed throughout the entire apartment. It was so bad that I knew there was no hiding it. Waiting another minute or two to answer the door would accomplish nothing. So I grabbed the doorknob and threw open the door.

"Good evening, Mr. Donovan," I said, smiling a wide grin as I looked at the balding gentleman standing before me. Next to him stood a relatively young woman, about twenty-five years of age, with blond hair and an attractive smile. Mr. Donovan wore a smile as well.

I tried my best to extend a cheery salutation to my visitors, which was difficult given the fact that I was being tortured from the inside out. By now, I felt like one of the hot air balloons you'd see in the Macy's Thanksgiving Day parade. If anything, it was still getting worse. As I stood there in my methane-inflated stance, I witnessed an amazing transition take place on the faces of my visitors. Their smiles, which were previously wide and genuine, became fixed as though they had been carved in stone. Their eyes both held expressions of alarm as they looked rapidly from floor to ceiling, trying to determine the source of the gas. Yet neither one of them wanted to back out of the tour, so in the door they came.

As they walked in the doorway and started the tour in the kitchen, Mr. Donovan went into his sales pitch, showing off the dishwasher, stove, and other modern appliances. He was trying to talk quickly, which was made tougher by the fact that he was holding his breath. At least partway, anyway. He wasn't breathing through his nose at all, and I noticed that his potential tenant had also decided to avoid that form of respiration. As a matter of fact, I have no proof that she was breathing at all, instead deciding to delay that bodily function until leaving the apartment. I really couldn't blame her.

To Mr. Donovan's credit, he didn't cut the tour short, but instead led his prospect through the entire place, focusing on the extra high windows and the conveniently situated bedroom. I don't know how much more than that he mentioned, as I had to run back to the bathroom and reseed the acrid cloud of gas. It just couldn't have gotten any worse.

By the time they wrapped up and walked back down the hallway, they were both suffering from oxygen deprivation. I don't think the woman had taken a breath since she walked in the door, and I noticed signs of a blue tinge creeping into her cheeks. Mr. Donovan himself was turning a fine shade of green, which was accentuated by the film of sweat that had broken out on top of his head. I considered asking them both whether they needed assistance, but decided against it. I had clearly done enough to create this problem and didn't want to aggravate it further in any way.

Needless to say, the woman decided not to rent the apartment next to ours, much to the dismay of our landlord. It wouldn't have surprised me if she had decided to move out of the neighborhood, although I never did hear of her final plans. As for me, I proceeded to open as many windows as I could find, then leave the apartment for the rest of the evening. Unfortunately, there was no form of forced ventilation in the place, and there was little or no wind that day. As a result, the full dose of my exhaust fumes were still in residence when I returned later that night. I think that by that time they had also permeated the carpeting and furniture upholstery. It was not a good scene.

It was around eleven-thirty when Patty returned from work, tired from a day full of running around after doctors and performing laboratory tests. It was her place, and she just wanted to relax before turning in. Unfortunately, relaxing means being able to breathe, which was still very difficult in that atmosphere.

"Good grief, what is that smell?" she gagged, as she staggered through the doorway. She was choked up, and I believe her eyes were beginning to water.

I did my best to explain, which failed to make matters any better. I admitted that Mr. Donovan's tour had probably been a washout, and that my own stock with Mr. Donovan had probably sunken to new lows. (He never approved of me staying with Patty on my days off anyway, and this latest episode would undoubtedly reinforce that position.)

This story does have a happy ending, because we were able to clear the air in the apartment that night by enlisting the help of a large window fan, which we ran for several hours. Within a week, Mr. Donovan had rented the adjacent apartment to a different tenant, although he wisely decided to complete the repairs and then show that apartment instead of asking to use Patty's.

As for me, I trashed the other two boxes of Indian Dinner, electing to leave them in the garbage pail rather than carry them into the woods. Even if nobody else was in residence in the area, I had too much respect for the flora and fauna of the West Canada Lakes Wilderness region to risk destroying it in such a manner. Instead, I opted for a package of good old fashioned franks and beans, which simply never tasted so good.

—20—

Out to Sea

"It will be good for him; they'll straighten him out and get him going in the right direction!"

These are words you'd expect to hear when addressing a derelict, bum, or juvenile delinquent. However, as I strode from the Department of Environmental Conservation District 10 Head-quarters building that afternoon, it felt quite unsettling that those words were meant for me. No, they weren't meant for me to hear, but there was no doubt that I was the subject of the argument, and it didn't feel good.

It was the end of the 1981 ranger season, and I was walking out the door of the DEC building for the last time. I had been through there countless times over the last three seasons, having left a few tons of my sweat and blood back in the woods. I felt as though I was a highly dedicated and devoted employee who had always done what was asked, and done it well. So why did I deserve this kind of treatment?

I called back that very same afternoon and spoke with my good friend Delos Mallette, who was the District Forester and "head honcho" in that office. My inquiries into the remark were met with a characteristic laugh from Delos, who went on to disarm my concerns.

"Oh, don't think twice about that," he said in a cheery voice. "It wasn't meant like that at all. It's just that Lynn is from the old school and looks at anyone with long hair in a suspicious light. Don't worry; everyone around here knows you've done a great job. Believe me, we're going to miss you."

His comments did in fact make me feel much better. After all, Lynn and I had always gotten along very well, and he had even volunteered to complete one of the recommendations I needed in order to apply for Navy Officer Candidate School (OCS). But there was no doubt that his assessment of my overall standing as a citizen of our fair country was affected by my appearance. After all, I had shoulder-length hair and a beard, whereas he resembled a Marine drill instructor. My ranger uniform (which was usually quite ready for the cleaners by the time I emerged from the woods each week) didn't add to my persona. There was no doubt that I looked like a less-than-desirable individual who would benefit from boot camp, and he seemed more than happy to help me get there.

Looking back on the whole thing, I'm amazed that I ever ended up in that situation at all. I say that because, in general, I am a person of routines. It is seldom that I am truly inspired by a new idea, instead preferring to stick with the same agenda I've followed for years. So it honestly surprised a lot of my friends and co-workers when I announced my decision to head off to OCS following the 1981 ranger season.

Those who knew me well, though, realized that this was not the first time I'd considered pursuing a career as a naval officer. In my earlier books on this topic, I mentioned that I had taken the admission exam for OCS as early as 1977. I was accepted, but I declined my appointment in order to attend graduate school in Syracuse. To this day, I am still glad that I made that decision, as it led directly to my job as a wilderness park ranger in the West

Canada Lakes region.

The decision to retake that OCS exam was something that I mulled over for much of the 1981 ranger season. It started with a chance visit to an old Navy recruiting station in Glens Falls. It was located in a dilapidated strip mall which was noteworthy only in its downtrodden appearance. The fading paint and dirty windows of the recruiting store bore testimony to the low budget approach imposed on the local recruiting station. It didn't look too appealing, although it did appear to have a moderate flow of interested young men and women stopping in to talk.

The person who helped me in that station was a Navy Chief, who obviously wanted to recruit as many individuals as possible in order to meet his quota. But he seemed genuinely interested in me and my career path, although he was somewhat amused at the career change I'd soon undertake.

"Well, it's going to be a lot different than living in the woods," he laughed, "although you're probably one of the few people who might enjoy the Navy racks more than your current sleeping arrangements." (The term "rack" means a bunk on a Navy ship.) Little did he know how much I loved sleeping on the floor of an Adirondack lean-to, with the sounds of the forest peeping through the night. I'd have taken that over any bed in the world.

The Chief spoke to me several times that summer when I returned to the office on my "weekends" to discuss Navy options. To me, it was one of the most exciting jobs I could think of as a follow-up to my current occupation. I also knew that there was little or no chance of moving up from the wilderness park ranger position to something that would be more permanent. The people who served as actual DEC forest rangers had to go through a long hiring process, starting with the Civil Service test and then on through a long battery of interviews and other exams. By comparison, the Navy seemed like a much more rapid and accessible career path.

As I hiked my way through the summer of 1981, I debated this choice at least a hundred times; should I sign up, or should I pursue other options? I was filled with uncertainties that wouldn't go away. After all, I had just spent three years living the ideal life of self-dependence. As long as I met my boss' schedule, I did as I pleased and lived according to my daily desires. I could go fishing whenever the urge struck me, sleep as long as I wanted, and live inside the prettiest forest anywhere. (This is my own opinion, granted, but I still believe it is true.) I would go from seeing my boss two or three times a year to being crammed into a ship with hundreds (or even thousands) of other seafaring men. Was this what I really wanted?

The answer, I soon decided, was yes. I was ready to move on to something that would allow me to advance in life, give me some management experience, and hopefully allow me to see some parts of the world I'd never seen. All of this was at my fingertips. As a matter of fact, I really didn't even have to change much about my clothing, as I had already been in uniform for three years, I was simply exchanging one for another. And all I had to do was to raise my right hand and agree to serve for a term of four years.

I've got to admit that my parents weren't the biggest supporters of my decision to join the Navy. This was a bit odd, since they were both big fans of the naval service. Long before I was born, my mother and father used to host naval games inside the basement of our New Jersey home. They, in conjunction with their friends, had modeled large collections of U.S. and foreign naval vessels, which they used to enact complex battle scenarios. The floor tiles were a uniform size, which was translated into a set scale for purposes of movement and weapons range. It was all done in realistic manner by groups of their friends who shared their passion in naval matters.

Regardless of their zeal for this game, they regarded my pending career change with trepidation. After all, they were concerned about the possibility that I would be going into harm's way, which is always worrisome to a loving parent. They had both spent their entire careers as highly educated professionals, both with advanced degrees,[5] and they expected that their children would follow in their footsteps. I often wonder how many of their gray hairs were a direct result of my unconventional and somewhat hazardous career path. Quite a few, I imagine. But I wasn't about to let that get in the way of my dream, so away I went.

About the only thing standing in my way of gaining another seat at OCS were the admission tests, which were given on a regular basis at numerous testing sites around the state. I was several years beyond college and had probably forgotten a lot of my advanced mathematics. Not that I ever excelled in that topic anyway, as complex formulas and equations always left me a bit befuddled. But I still refused to study for the tests, as I simply didn't want to spend my evenings in the woods staring at the "cheat sheet" guides that were available from the bookstores. No, I would live dangerously and wing it. And if my scores didn't come up to their standards, then they'd just have to do without me!

In retrospect, I'm glad that I didn't spend any extra time preparing for the exams, as I passed with flying colors. My math and verbal scores both exceeded the minimum requirements by quite a bit, and even my mechanical aptitude test resulted in an outstanding score. I personally found that to be rather amusing, as the words "Some Assembly Required" printed on the outside of a package have always sent shivers up my spine. I'm amazed by the people who enjoy putting together their own bicycles and Bar-B-Q grills, being blessed with those innate skills that passed over me at birth.

The only part of the OCS test I didn't "ace" was the part I didn't take, which was for aviation and flight. It was the last of the four parts of the test, and when I turned to that page of the

<hr/>

[5] My father, Dr. Carol E. Weill, was a Ph.D. chemist, and was Chairman of the Chemistry Department of Rutgers University, Newark campus. My mother, Bernice Weill, had a Master's Degree and was a learning disability specialist and a published author.

exam, I simply put down my pencil and prepared to leave. The officer in charge of the proctoring the exam gave me a level stare and asked me about my actions.

"Don't you want to take the test to become a pilot," he inquired? "You never know; you might do really well."

I told him that I had no intention of ever, EVER flying my own plane. If I was going to take off to get from Point A to Point B, someone else was going to be sitting in the pilot's seat, because I'd be in row 7 eating my tiny bag of complimentary pretzels, thank you very much! He didn't seem overly impressed with my answer, but then again he couldn't make me take that section, which would have been pointless since I didn't want to fly.

My scores on the test were sent directly to my officer recruiter, who was located in Albany, New York. He was a Lieutenant Commander and a Navy nurse, although he was currently assigned to perform a year or two of recruiting duty at that station. I found him to be both friendly and knowledgeable, which were very comforting as I went through the process of scheduling an actual date to start OCS.

Actually, there were one or two other requirements that I had to fulfill in order to gain acceptance into the program. One of these was a formal interview with a two-officer panel. My recruiter served as one of those officers, while a newly-commissioned Ensign filled in as the second member. I'm not really certain whether anyone has ever been rejected at this point in the process, but our session went extremely well. We discussed my goals in life and my views on the world and on leadership and authority. Not much of my life in the woods translated into usable skills for my new career, although we did strike a common bond on more than one topic.

"I'm not really motivated by financial reward," I remember saying, referring to my wonderful wage of four dollars and twenty-seven cents an hour. "I need to know that I am performing as part of a team, and that my job and my actions will help us accomplish our mission."

That struck a real cord with my hosts, who were amused at my level of compensation. "Oh, you won't get rich serving in the Navy," said the Commander, "but you will make a lot more than you're making now. I can guarantee you that in writing."

I left the woods that year in late September, stopping for a few days in Glens Falls before heading south to Albany for my swearing-in ceremony. I had already decided to put off the start date for OCS until early February of the following year, as there were some other issues to handle before reporting for duty in uniform. But regardless of my report date, I still wanted to take the oath as soon as possible, which meant right after leaving the woods in 1981.

I still have the photographs of myself standing in front of the American flag, one hand raised while solemnly taking the oath. Another photo shows me smiling while shaking hands with the recruiter, as a yeoman stands by with the paperwork for me to sign. In both shots, I am dressed in a rather worn-out woolen sweater that had accompanied me throughout my days in the woods. Its sleeves had small holes where my elbows had worn through the coarse fibers, and the neckline was stretched out of shape by the weight of my pack's shoulder straps. My hair was cropped back somewhat to a more manageable mane, but still looked as though it could use a good trimming.

None of this concerned me at the time, though, as I was merely raising my hand for future service. I knew that I need not bother with getting a haircut now, as I wouldn't be reporting for OCS for another four months. Once that time arrived, the Navy would take care of everything. They'd give me a haircut, they'd give me a uniform, and they'd provide me with anything else I needed.

In fact, I had no doubt in my mind that no matter what I looked like when I reported for duty, the Navy would straighten me out and get me heading in the right direction.

—21—

Two Decades Later

Although my last year in the woods as a ranger was 1981, I never forgot the beauty of the land and lakes or the sounds of the woods around me. These natural phenomena became ingrained in my soul, and will forever be a part of who I am.

The years since my ranger experience have been very rewarding, although I have never enjoyed my surroundings as I did back then. After spending four years on active duty with the Navy and then continuing that career in the Reserves, I turned my hand to writing and instructing. I worked for Xerox Corporation for many years after my naval service, and there I learned how to survive in the "corporate jungles" that were so very different from my woodsy past.

As the years flew by and my memories of the West Canada days began to gradually recede, they were replaced by equally rewarding experiences in my new and growing family. In 1994, our daughter Kelly was born. She would later be joined in 2002 by a sister, Erin. The addition of these youngsters to our happy family has been the crowning point of my life, and we have since started bringing them along on our recent Adirondack visits.

Through all of these turns in my life, the thought of making a return to the West Canadas kept poking its way into my mind. It wasn't something that I was actively planning, but I did find myself often daydreaming about the shores of West Lake. I wondered about the trails and the lean-tos, the hidden boats and the old camps. How had they changed with the passage of time? What would I recognize of the old landscape, and what would appear new?

After briefly considering a return visit through my old territory, I quickly formed a number of excuses to prevent me from actually making the trip. I knew that several of the old-timers were now gone, which would provide a sad reminder of yesteryear. Leighton Slack and John Remias had both passed away, and (to the best of my knowledge) none of my old friends were back there on the trail crew. The tower on Pillsbury was vacant, as were all of the towers in the state.

Another factor in postponing this trip was my physical condition. In the years since working in the woods, I had developed arthritis in my right hip, which was perhaps initiated by the rough life on the trail. This condition was getting progressively worse, which would make hiking with a load difficult. I knew that it would someday have to be replaced, although I was putting this off as long as I could. Would the creaky old hip joint tolerate a heavy pack and uneven trails? I didn't know.

All of these factors were jostling about in my mind as I conducted my internal debate: should I return for another visit or should I pass on the idea? I was sitting at my desk at Xerox one lunch hour in the spring of 2000 considering this very issue when the phone rang. It was David, one of my best friends from my early days of high school. David and I had shared a lot of good times over the years, and we had remained in touch both through college and later as we entered our current jobs. I trusted David as much as anyone and had given him an advanced copy of my first Adirondack manuscript to read. I knew that, as always, Dave would give me an honest opinion on my work. He was just that kind of person. It was good to hear from him.

"I've got a good idea," he began. "But I don't know if you're up to it."

"Well, why don't you tell me about it," I replied. "I don't think I can comment unless you tell me what you're thinking."

"I was wondering if you'd like to take me on a trip back through your old ranger district," he said. "After reading your manuscript, I've been curious about seeing it. I've got some time off coming next month and wanted to see if you'd be willing to take a hike."

The question came like an electric shock to me, and I quickly confessed that I had been mulling over these same thoughts for at least a year or so. We readily agreed on a date later in the summer and put it on our calendars. Based on the enthusiasm that I felt for the venture, I knew that it was the right thing to do and that Dave would be great company on the trails. He confessed to having a few aches and pains of his own, so the two of us would hobble through the woods together.

We agreed to meet in Speculator on the night of August 16, 2000, and stay overnight in a hotel before hitting the trail. Dave would be driving up from New Jersey while I was coming in from western New York. Hopefully, our rendezvous would allow us an early start the following morning.

By the time Dave arrived, it was almost midnight, which meant that we'd be getting a reduced night's sleep; not a problem, as neither of us really required a lot. However, that was before the pillows started flying across the room from one bed to the other.

"Hey...Larry....wake up! You're snoring like a locomotive," Dave cried! "I hope that's not your normal volume; I'll never get any sleep this week!"

I had to admit that it was, as I have never been a silent sleeper. But it didn't take long for both of us to fall asleep readily, anticipating getting an early start the following morning.

After a quick breakfast and packing session, we headed off to Perkins Clearing, ready to start our journey. I purposefully avoided going down to see whether Leighton's cabin was still standing below the clearing. The endless cups of coffee, the games of horseshoes, and the hours of earnest conversation were among my favorite memories of my years in the West Canadas, and I was sorry that he was gone. I really had no need or desire to see his empty cabin, or to see the place where it once stood.

The trip in to Sled Harbor went quickly, and we parked the car in an open area. As I saddled up in my pack, a flood of emotions washed over me. This felt so familiar, yet so distant. I had lived this life five days a week in a different time. So much had changed, yet so much felt the same.

One thing that hadn't changed was the weight of my pack. "Oooomph," I heard myself groan, as I pulled the load up onto my back. I adjusted the hip straps...a lot, for they were pulled into position to ride on a much smaller person. (That much smaller person had been me, and I wasn't too happy about that fact.)

As I pulled my canteen onto my hip strap, I thought about the other new device that I was carrying—the water filter. I had never needed a filter in my days living back there. I'd just dip my canteen into any old stream or source of running water, and voila, I was ready. But not now. On an earlier visit, in the mid 1980s, I had asked Leighton whether I could fill my canteen from the brook in back of his house. He cautioned me about the new "bug" that had infested the waters and said that I'd have to boil the water. That bug turned out to be the *Giardia lamblia* that we've all come to know, which can cause extreme intestinal distress if not properly filtered or treated. After that, I had purchased a high-end filtration system, although I had never used it prior to this trip.

It was late morning by the time we hit the trail. We received our first test of strength and stamina quite early. The first two to three miles take you straight up Blue Ridge, which is otherwise known as "Sonofabitch Hill." (This nickname requires little or no explanation.) As we approached the start of the incline, I wondered whether I was up to the task. Out of shape and overweight, I hadn't done anything like this in a long time. David confessed to being out of shape as well, so we'd be moving kind of slow. Yet, despite my concerns, we did OK. By keeping our minds off of the hill and on our conversation, the miles quickly fell away. Yes, our breath was labored, and yes, I was using my walking stick to pull me up the ascent. But it was going as well as could be expected. Soon, amazingly soon, we were standing at the top of the ridge at the junction of the paths to Pillsbury and Cedar Lakes. I was overjoyed, knowing that this week would be physically "endurable" for both of us. Not bad for a couple of old timers!

The next few miles, which would take us across Grassy Brook and on to Cedar Lakes, did seem to be longer than I remembered. Several landmarks that I had used as reference points were now gone, such as large trees that had been cut out of the trail and lengthy stretches of "corduroy" logs which had been laid to keep the mud and water at bay. I also noticed that at least one new bridge had been built over a creek that would have otherwise presented an impassable obstacle. It was nice to see that some trail work was still being performed on critical areas.

As we approached the land near Cedar Lakes, I found myself looking forward to seeing the old dam. The bridge over the dam had collapsed several years earlier, so I was not expecting to see that. However, as we emerged from the trees and caught our first glimpse of the lake, I was happy to see that the dam itself was still intact.

We passed the spot where the first Cedar Lakes lean-to had stood, and I had to take a break. I took my pack off and walked around the old site. It was obvious that a lot of folks still used this as a tent site, and the ground was devoid of plant life where the lean-to had once stood.

This was a very sentimental place for me. It marked the place where I slept on both my first and last nights as a ranger in the West Canada Lakes. I could not count the number of friends I'd made at that spot, the number of fires I'd sat around, and the number of stories told over those fires. Dave watched me as I just stood there and stared at the land, listening to the ghosts of the past as they floated back in my memories. I could have listened for hours and still not have heard or recalled all of the voices from across the years.

We decided to head off and see whether we could get a lean-to, since it was still fairly early in the day. The first lean-to was the new one that had been built as a replacement for the original structure by the dam. It had been erected near the site of the old Cedar Lakes caretaker's cabin, in an overgrown clearing that had been part of the cabin's front yard.

It took us only a few minutes to arrive at this lean-to, which we found to be empty. I had never stayed at this new structure, and I found it to be rather impersonal. Strange as it sounds, each of the lean-tos in the West Canadas had taken on its own personality over the years, and I had developed a particular affinity for certain ones over the rest. This new lean-to, which was small and seemingly sterile, offered nothing at all in the way of "friendly vibrations."

I turned to Dave and gave him our options. "Well, we have a choice," I said. "We can stay here and have a guaranteed lean-to to ourselves, or we can mosey on down the trail and see if the Beaver Pond lean-to is open."

Dave was quick to offer an opinion. "Beaver Pond is the place you were talking about last night, right? The place with the overlook from the hill, with the nice spring and the loons nearby?"

"Yup, that's the one," I replied. "In my opinion, it's about the nicest place around here, bar none."

"Well, what are we waiting for?" Dave asked. "We might as well get moving before someone else sets up shop down there."

I readily agreed, although I found that I had grown quite comfortable in my prone position on the floor of the new lean-to. It is funny what old age can do to you!

With a small amount of grunting and groaning, we both heaved on our packs and got ready for the final half-mile trek to Beaver Pond, which involved a few steep uphill and downhill scampers. As we crested the final hilltop and started our descent towards the lake, I was happy to see that there were no signs of anyone camping at the lean-to. No smoke was drifting up from the fireplace, and (even at a distance) I could see no visible signs of clothing hanging from the front of the lean-to.

Our gamble paid off; it was empty, and we quickly spread our belongings out across the floorboards of the structure. It was approaching the later half of the afternoon and we still had not seen another hiker. This was ideal!

As we rolled out our sleeping bags and foam pads, I discovered something about being a forty-five year old hiker instead of a twenty-five year old hiker. I discovered naps. Funny, but I had never taken a nap when I worked back here as a ranger. Yet as I rolled out my pad and sleeping bag, there was a tangible force which grabbed me and pulled me down onto my bedding. I had never noticed how soft and comfortable that bag could be after a hike into the woods. Within ten minutes, I was sound asleep.

I'm not sure just what it was that brought me out of my slumber, but I quickly looked at my watch and found that I'd been out for about two hours. Looking across the lean-to, I noticed that David had followed my lead and was also down for the count. Ha! So I wasn't the only one who had been caught by the fickle finger of aging.

Oh well, it was now approaching dinner hour, so I figured that I'd head out and try to pull in some firewood. This was something that I always enjoyed, and I was generally able to bring in some pretty nice hauls within a short period of time. Based on my initial trip, I judged that a lot of storms must have passed through that summer, for it took me very little effort to locate some out-standing stashes of wood. As I stacked the limbs and shouldered them for the return trip to the lean-to, I wondered whether I could do this again on a full-time basis. Pointless question, of course, but still I wondered. What a great way to get back into shape!

I rounded the front of the lean-to and dumped the wood in a single heave. It made a rather mighty crash as it hit the ground, which awakened David with a start. He gave the wood a quick glance from the corner of his eye, which seemed to remind him of his current position.

"Hey! You want help with that stuff?" he asked, pushing him-self up to a sitting position.

"No, I don't mind getting it myself," I replied. "But I'll tell you what—how about you break this stuff up into fireplace-sized pieces while I get another load or two. We should be ready to cook dinner within a half hour."

We agreed on this division of labor and quickly built a wood pile that would last us through the night. Meanwhile, I found some birch paper and some other small kindling and built the fire pile until it was ready to light. As I did during all my years in the woods as a ranger, I still preferred cooking over a real fire, but as I did then, I carried a stove and fuel on this trip in case we had any rainy days.

Since I had done all of the food shopping and packing myself, I had decided to make life easy on us and bring along mostly dehydrated food packs. Sure, I know, a lot of hikers prefer to carry in all of the gourmet ingredients and really do it up on short trips of three or four days. However, I think that my deci-sion was tempered by the fact that we were no longer youngsters who could pack in all the extra weight required to do that kind of cooking. No, dehydrated food sounded great to me, and we quickly made our menu selections based on the choices that I pulled from my pack.

Not bad stuff! Our entrees were lasagna and Taiwanese chicken and noodles. It is still amazing just how great some of that stuff can taste after you've been on the trail all day. It didn't take long to polish off the two meals, along with a healthy supply of dinner rolls. Life was good!

The next few hours sort of flashed past, as we cleaned up and got ready to enjoy the evening colors from the Western skies. I had always loved this lean-to on Beaver Pond, and tonight, as I looked down at the fish jumping at the surface near the cattail reeds, very little seemed to have changed. The same breeze came up and pushed the water into ripples as it flowed under the Beaver Pond bridge, and the customary loons soon made their appearance. It was nothing short of magical, and I sat spellbound watching the scenery unfold.

Once the sun went down, the temperature dropped quite quickly, and I was glad for the extra gloves and hat that I had packed for the two of us. We talked for another hour or two as we sat on the front of the lean-to, watching the fire dance around the stone fireplace. The latter half of August was always a great time of year, because most of the "night bugs" were gone (although they could still be a nuisance during the day), and the cold weather hadn't really taken hold. We savored every moment until the sky turned completely black, after which we turned in for the night. To this moment, we still hadn't seen another soul since leaving Speculator.

We awakened fairly early the following morning, due in large part to the cool temperatures that begged us to get up and about. I climbed out of the sleeping bag and rapidly revived our fire from the previous evening. Hot chocolate is great for warming up the inner being, so I quickly heated some water and prepared two steaming mugs of the beverage. I also discovered that, after my nineteen-year hiatus, I could once again eat oatmeal! Good thing, too, as that was about all that I'd brought along for our morning meals.

David and I both had only four days in which to complete this trip before heading back to our offices, so I decided on a route that would take us through the West Canadas as far as South Lake today. Then, on Saturday, we'd leave the Northville-Lake Placid Trail and head off toward Sampson Lake. From there, it would be onward to Pillsbury Lake for our final night in the woods. On Sunday morning we'd wrap it up with a short five-mile trek back to the clearing next to Sled Harbor. It sounded like a good plan, so we prepared to break camp and head off westward on the day's hike.

As we headed west, I was amazed at how little had changed. The wet areas were still wet, the same landmark trees were still in place, and all else appeared to be intact after the passage of two decades. It was a walk back into my past, and I stopped often to point out features to my friend. Many times I found myself laughing at things that had happened at various points along the trail, and I even saw a few instances of my own handi-work that were still in place. Time moves slowly in the woods, and I was glad for that fact.

As we approached the West Canadas, the trail suddenly took a major detour, and the old route to which I was accustomed was blocked off. It was a huge reroute, and I could see that it had been in place for about a year or so. In an instant I figured out what had happened. The beavers which had played havoc with the low-lying wetlands around Mud Lake had finally won the war, and the state had conceded the fight. The new trail appeared to circumvent the entire area, heading off on a tangent that would take it much farther away from the lake. Unfortunately, as with all new trails, this one was very rough and rigorous, with numer-ous pits and treacherous openings that gaped between the tree roots. It was difficult footing, and one false step could have taken my rickety old hip and wrenched it loose. It took a long time to go the next mile, and we found ourselves glad when the trail rejoined the old route on the other side of the wetland.

But only for a couple hundred yards.

As we headed through the final stand of timber leading up to West Lake, I found my heart pounding. I was about to see something that I did not want to see. It was the old clearing marking the site of the caretaker's cabin, which had been burned out years earlier. It was a sight that I knew would sadden me, and I steeled myself for its appearance.

We emerged from the brush and looked west toward the lake. It was nothing like I imagined, and I found myself stunned to the soul. Not only was the cabin gone, but the entire landscape was different. The clearing that had been John's front yard was gone. I mean, *it was completely gone!* I had heard about the speed with which trees will grow back over a burned area, but this was just plain crazy.

I walked forward into the pile of rubble that had been John's home. It was nothing but bricks and rocks, seared from the heat of the fire and tossed randomly about the site. It was all that was left of the old foundation. In front of that pile was a solid line of trees that completely obscured any view of the lake. To anyone who had never been there before, it was as though the lawn had never existed. I had been prepared for some extensive thickets, and maybe a few small saplings, but nothing like this.

For the second time in two days, Dave watched as I silently surveyed the remains of my past. Ghosts were speaking to me, and I was trying to hear. I felt the red brick cinders crunch beneath my feet as I walked slowly around the ruins. As I paced, I recreated the old cabin in my mind. Here would have been the fireplace in the living room, so the wood burning stove would have been about here. Turning around, I envisioned the chair where John sat by the window and the table at which he ate his meals. It was all there in spirit, and I took my time as I felt the presence of these things in my mind. There wasn't anything to say, yet there was so much to feel.

As I continued to look around, David took some photographs. He was interested in the cross that someone had produced and left on the site as a memorial. "You did not conform" was the epilogue etched onto the artifact, a testimonial to the senseless burning of the beautiful building. I too examined the cross, although I did not dwell on it. The house was gone, John was gone, and nothing was going to change any of that.

Looking into the new growth of trees, I was relieved to see that the fireplace built by French Louis had been left intact, although it was already being hidden somewhat by the trees. I hoped that enough people knew of its significance that they would continue to keep it cleared from brush in the coming years. It is far too famous to become obscured and forgotten, although these same words have probably been uttered about other now-forgotten landmarks as well. As I examined it up close, I was saddened to see that none of French Louis' snakes still slithered around its base, hoping (all these generations later) for his return. Perhaps they were merely napping under a rock or sunning themselves in a more secluded location. I know that both Louis and John would hope so, and thus so did I.

After spending a solemn half hour on the site, we decided to head off towards our destination for the day and set up camp. The West Lake lean-to was empty, which meant that we could stop right there and have a place to ourselves. However, just like the previous day, we decided to risk it and head off to check out a better spot. The South Lake lean-to has always been a favorite in our area due to the white sand beach and the spectacular sunsets. So why not? We decided to go for it.

Another half mile of hiking and we pulled into the clearing that surrounded South Lake, that beautiful stretch of water that lay just to the south of West Lake. It was as we had hoped— empty, with no trace of humans in the area. We quickly staked our claim and moved in.

Once we opened up our packs and arranged our pads and sleeping bags, we noticed a suspicious pattern creeping in. It served as confirmation of the previous day's events and a reminder of our advancing age. Yup—the call of the sleeping bag became loud and clear, and we once again agreed that a nap was the order of the afternoon. This time, we had arrived earlier in the day and thus felt no need to limit ourselves to a short catnap. As such, the duration of our slumber was longer, and we slept until the later part of the afternoon. I knew that this was something I never would have done in my twenties, but it all seemed so natural (even necessary) now. I was no longer a spring chicken.

The wood gathering and meal preparation was a simple repeat of the prior day. Since we had no spring nearby, I had to break out the new filtration device, which we used to siphon water right out of the lake. I've got to admit that I didn't trust the little hose-like device much, especially since the consequences of failure would have been an extended stay on the outhouse throne. But all went well with its setup and use, and we were soon on our way with the meal.

True to form, we ate and cleaned our dishes while watching the onset of another gorgeous South Lake sunset. It was one of my favorite places in the woods, and I was glad to have the chance to return this one time with such a good friend. And all this transpired without seeing another hiker. We had been out for two days and had yet to see anyone. It felt like home.

The next morning we broke camp and headed south over West Canada Creek, then turned back to the East. The plan was to make it past Sampson and Whitney Lakes and camp out at Pillsbury Lake, which was the location of another one of French Louis' larger camps. Pillsbury was a scenic place, and yet for all my time in these woods I had only slept there a handful of times. My weekly schedule as a ranger took me past there almost every week but almost never allowed me to stop and spend the night. So this would be somewhat novel even for me.

The two of us slogged on ahead, up the rise of land that lead us towards Sampson Lake. This stretch of trail was never used as much as the rest of the territory because it is not part of the

Northville-Lake Placid Trail. In general, only the local folks used it, or those hikers who wanted to visit West Canada Lake by the shortest possible access route from Speculator. (Anyone traveling from Indian Lake and north could get in to West Lake in a day from the Moose River Plains, but we seldom saw anyone using that route.) I was glad to see Dave stopping occasionally for a breather, as it benefited my own legs and lungs as well.

We passed the turnoff for the Sampson Lake lean-to and continued on without stopping. I started to look for some rocky outcroppings I knew as landmarks, but instead found my view to be completely obstructed. This trail had received very little in the way of attention over the past few years and was greatly overgrown. I took the lead so that I could be sure that we were still following the trail at all. At times, we were pushing through undergrowth that completely closed off the trail and met in the middle, thus requiring me to look to the ground for confirmation that we were still on track.

I was slightly angered by this negligence, and I found myself wishing that I could voice my opinion to the state about these conditions. However, I quickly realized that there was nobody left back here to handle this kind of maintenance, and that these smaller trails may soon have to become just another casualty in the budget wars of the state. As sad as it seemed, the older maps were full of trails that no longer existed even when I was a ranger. Perhaps this was the standard way in which they died, left to grow their way into obscurity. As with French Louis' fireplace, I fervently wished that some of the local sportsmen who continued to follow these trails would come through with a machete and reopen them for use, but I didn't have much hope.

It wasn't long before we passed the hidden beauty of Whitney Lake, and the trail opened up into the muddy strip that had once been a drivable lane. It was very wet, with evidence of beaver work in the area, but it was quite passable. I noticed with some satisfaction that some of the "camp trash" that had been visible along this route was now either hidden or completely removed. One or two of the large camps in the vicinity of Whitney had their contents removed and littered throughout the woods, including a few major appliances and other eyesores. None of these were still in evidence as we headed along the road in route to Pillsbury. And while this part of the walk still held for me some degree of sentimentality, it also had the distinct feeling of being less wild, as though we were approaching the outskirts of the wilderness.

We arrived at the turnoff for the Pillsbury Lake lean-to and headed off down the path towards the old shelter. As with the other lean-tos (except the first one on Cedar Lakes), it was an original from my days as a ranger. It was also empty, so we once again claimed squatter's rights and moved in.

Another nap. By now it seemed natural. However, after only an hour I was awakened by the sound of jingling metal, which I quickly recognized as dogs tags on a chain collar. True to my guess, a rather large hound dog of questionable lineage poked its way around the corner of the lean-to and looked inside. A quick "Hello, pup" from me brought a single bark in reply, before the dog bolted away from the lean-to. I knew that its owner was certainly nearby, and my assumption was quickly confirmed.

Within a minute, a young man in his early twenties walked around the front of the lean-to and looked at us suspiciously. I don't know why, but he didn't look like someone who could be trusted. Call it a sixth sense, but I just felt it inside.

"How ya doing?" I asked, sitting up and moving to the front of the lean-to. "Nice looking dog you've got there."

"Thanks. I was just doing some fishing. Caught some nice ones down at Whitney earlier today."

I nodded in acknowledgement, saying that we had just come that way ourselves. I didn't bother to tell him that I hadn't seen anyone's footprints along the trail, thus making his story all the more questionable. However, this was not my problem, and as long as he wasn't going to make any trouble, he could claim that he caught Moby Dick for all I cared. He soon left, and I watched him as he retreated up the trail that would lead him back to town.

Dave and I spent our last afternoon gathering wood and getting ready for the evening meal and fire. Good hardwood was a little bit harder to find around here, as the entire area around the lean-to was dominated by spruce and other soft woods. But a short hike back to the main road yielded a healthy supply of maple and beech, which we used to build a large stockpile inside the lean-to. That was part of the "Code of the Woods," and I always tried to obey its unwritten law. I had made it a personal habit of leaving a significant pile of dry wood when I left a site, and my last night here would be no different.

Sundown over Pillsbury is another beautiful sight, as the water around the rocky outcroppings to the west reflects a wonderful pallet of color into the back of the lean-to. The sun always seems to set quite slowly there, which gave us a lengthy and leisurely evening in which to spend our final hours in the woods. I found that I was doing a lot less reminiscing than expected, which was probably due to the fact that I hadn't spent much time at this particular site over the years. Our evening was spent comparing notes of our lives—where we had had similar experiences and where they had differed. I had known both of Dave's parents before they passed away, and he had known both of mine. (I am blessed to still have a mother in good health.) It was an enjoyable evening, which seemed to pass entirely too fast. It would be my last night in the woods for a very long time.

As with the previous evening, the temperature dropped rapidly once the sun went down. We threw a lot of extra wood on the fire, which we kept going much later than other nights that week. This would be the "grand finale" bonfire for the trip, and we continued to huddle up to its warmth as the stories were traded. It was several hours after dark and well down into the wood pile when we decided to turn in.

Unlike the first two nights of the trip, the air temperature continued to fall during the night. I pulled on my thermal long johns, along with the matching hat and gloves. Even with all these items layered on my body, I still found that I felt the chill as I hunkered down into my sleeping bag. It was a cold, cold night. I awakened several times and found myself looking out across the lake. The moonlight was quite bright, and I studied the opposite shoreline as I looked for signs of the coming dawn. It was too darned cold.

By the time I pulled the sleeping bag from over my face for the fourth or fifth time, the Eastern sky was turning gray, and I catapulted myself out of the bag. Wool jacket, heavier pants, windbreaker, the works! I threw clothes onto my body as quickly as I could pull them from the pack, shivering all the while. Was I really this out of shape, or could it be that it hadn't been as cold when I lived back here? I didn't know the answer to this, and I didn't care. (In retrospect, though, some of the coldest temperatures I ever experienced in the West Canada Lakes were in the vicinity of Pillsbury Lake, so perhaps I was justified in my opinion.) I had soon covered my body with an extra two or three layers of clothing and was doing my best imitation of the Michelin Man.

Our final walk out of the woods was uneventful, although we did pass by two or three groups of hikers who were off to various destinations both near and far. I found it hard to believe, but I had to fight the urge to question these folks about their destinations. I had an almost insatiable desire to provide directions and recommendations regarding their routes, which made no sense at all given the passage of time. However, this behavior had become so ingrained in me that I found it almost impossible to alter.

I kept my eyes locked forward and maintained my pace, placing one foot in front of the other. Larry the ranger has been gone for twenty years. Forget the past and just worry about making it back to the car in one piece. Left, right, left, right. Final mile of hiking and all is still well!

As we approached the clearing that surrounded Sled Harbor,

we broke out in a pair of wide grins. A few more steps and we launched ourselves into an acrobatic version of "high-fives." No, not that we hadn't expected to make it all the way through the week, although we had done so with fewer aches and pains than expected. And that in itself was an accomplishment.

For David, it was a chance to see all the wonders that I had described to him over the years. It was a look inside the vast expanses of wilderness that even most native New Yorkers never experience, the remote Adirondacks at their finest.

For me, it was a chance to revisit the past, to confirm that you can go back and that the important things do not change. It was a great opportunity to introduce a good friend to a natural wonder, while also saying goodbye to those same sights and places that I might never see again. It was chance to feel both youth and age at the same time, to look ahead yet still remember the past.

I was feeling pretty good by the time I took off my pack and loaded it into the car trunk. We had seen what we came to see, and we had survived it all with no real aches or pains worth mentioning. Not bad for a couple of old men.

—22—

Closing the Circle

Note to the reader—this chapter was written by my daughter, Kelly, following our journey through the West Canada Lakes in the summer of 2007. It is written as seen through her eyes, experiencing the wilderness of the Adirondack backcountry for the first time. Serving as a guide in this capacity, and observing the youthful exuberance of my daughter as she discovered this paradise, was one of the high points of my years in the woods. I hope you enjoy her story!

This was a little harder than I had imagined. Sure, as a typical American thirteen-year-old girl, I liked the outdoors and adventure. Since my father had briefed me for the rough conditions, I hadn't expected our trip into the West Canada Lakes to be glamorous. But now that we were hot, wet, dirty, and completely surrounded by biting insects, all of which seemed intent on draining my body of blood, the trip was a looking a little less enjoyable. Like I said, it wasn't the mental image I had when I first read my father's books on life in the West Canada Lakes.

The idea for this trip had come about several years earlier, when my father first proposed the idea of taking me back into his old ranger district. I had been extremely enthusiastic about seeing the woods that he had patrolled in his ranger days, some twenty-six years earlier. Now my wish was coming true.

The days leading up to our hike were filled with entirely too much activity. We had spent the past two weeks on vacation, so the details of packing for the trail were hardly foremost on my mind. I had lots do to, including packing my new water-resistant clothing and pushing my new ultra-lite (and ultra-warm) sleeping bag into the bottom of my oversized pack. It seemed like the "day of reckoning" was approaching all too quickly.

The alarm clock was set for a frightfully early hour on the morning of our departure. In order to arrive at Perkins Clearing by noon, we had to hold reveille at five-thirty, much earlier than I would have liked. It was so early, in fact, that Dad had to wake me three times before I actually got up.

As we drove east across the state, then north to the Adirondacks, the scenery changed dramatically. The deciduous trees were replaced by conifers, and more hills appeared. Shortly after we entered the park, we spotted a group of turkeys standing in the road. As they ran off at the sight of our car, it struck me that few cars had driven down this deserted road recently to scare them off.

Before we entered the woods, we stopped to visit Barb Remias, John Remias' widow. I was excited at the prospect of meeting a character from my dad's books. I liked Barb from the moment I met her. She and Dad talked about how the woods had changed since his ranger days. As they talked, Barb referred to John as having "left us too soon." Although he had been ill for a while, he had passed away rather suddenly, and he was still missed by the many people who loved him. They had fun talking, but we knew that we had many miles still to cover that day. Barbara wished us luck on our trip and we continued our drive to Perkins Clearing.

We made one final stop before hitting the trail: at Charlie John's store for lunch. As we ate our sandwiches, Dad pointed out that this was the last "real food" we'd eat for several days. On the trail, our meals would consist of granola bars, trail mix, and various dehydrated substances. I had to admit, the dehydrated meals looked pretty unappealing, and I had doubts that a bag of crunchy morsels could become "Jamaican Jerk Chicken" with the addition of a little hot water.

On Route 8, Dad pointed out a "Moose Crossing" sign. He explained that the swampy waters to our left were ideal moose territory. "That's where I'd live, if I were a moose," he joked. We looked carefully, but didn't spot anything. Soon we turned onto the logging road that led into the woods. Several tent sites could be seen from the road, and I laughed to myself as I was reminded of Dad's stories about Whitehouse, a similar site. Detouring onto another small road, Dad drove the car to Leighton Slack's old shack. It was still there and was being maintained, but nobody was home. I could tell that Dad would have liked nothing more than to go visit his old friend, but that was impossible, Leighton having passed away many years ago.

The logging road was lined with raspberry bushes on either side. We rolled down the window and grabbed a few berries but we couldn't stop, as Dad's car was clearly dying. It had 185,000 miles on the odometer, and it was making noises similar to that of a jet plane taking off. We didn't trust it enough to stop for long. Dad also pointed out several large, feathery birds scurrying into the bushes. "Those are partridges," he explained. "They can give you a heart attack if you don't know that they're nearby. They're very loud." We parked the car at Sled Harbor, where the trail began. There was only one other car parked there, and we spoke briefly to its driver, who was hiking Pillsbury alone.

Even on the wide and "drivable" trail, the woods were beautiful. As we hiked, Dad told me more about the area. "It gets pretty cold back here, even in early August," he informed me.

"The Pillsbury Lake lean-to always seems colder than the rest; it can get positively freezing at night, even in the summer." Wow! It sure was a good thing I brought my new jacket that we had bought especially for the trip! But the more I thought about the jacket, the less I was sure that I had packed it. For all I knew, it was still in my room back home. What if I hadn't brought it? Would I freeze at night? Finally, about a half mile down the trail, I spoke up. "You know, I don't think I remember where I packed that jacket," I said conversationally. Unfortunately, Dad saw right through my casual remark. "You don't have your jacket?" he asked. "Are you serious?" We opened my pack and began searching frantically for the garment. Eventually, I discovered it in a side compartment, and we were able to resume our hike with little time lost.

I had been dreading the hike up Blue Ridge (or "Sonofabitch Hill," as it was sometimes called), so it came as a surprise to me that it was not nearly as long or steep as I had expected. In fact, I made it up quite easily. At this point I felt slightly guilty: Dad's pack weighed over twice as much as mine. It contained our tent, stove, food, water pump, and other heavy supplies. I could only imagine how heavy it was. Still, I didn't feel guilty enough to volunteer to carry any of it!

We signed into the register at the bottom of Pillsbury Mountain. We were the only group backpacking, as everyone else was either day hiking to the Mountain or to Pillsbury Lake. Once we passed the register, the dirt road closed down to a trail. Dad told me that at one point, the trail had been a dirt road, too. He pointed out how quickly nature reclaimed itself, something that he would mention often during the trip. When we arrived at Grassy Brook, we found a very rickety bridge. Dad said that it was the third bridge he remembered in that particular spot. As it creaked underneath us, I couldn't help but wonder how the other two collapsed; I didn't really want to think about it.

It was somewhere near Grassy Brook when they first attacked:

deerflies, mosquitoes, and what seemed like every other kind of biting insect known to mankind swooped down upon us. Dad attempted to drive them away by swatting at them with his bandana. I found a different use for the bandana. I put it over my head and used it as a shield. This method seemed to work fairly well, as my face received very few bites. We hiked on, despite the cloud of insects that now swarmed around us. Dad told me that in another two weeks they'd all be gone, but that did little to improve the situation.

From there on, the trail became muddy and wet. Corduroy logs and tree stumps were placed strategically to "assist" you over particularly wet places. I decided against using these lethally slippery logs when I nearly fell into a puddle while hopping from stump to stump. To this day, I am convinced that the logs were placed back there as a cruel joke by someone who thought it would be funny to watch hikers fall into the mud.

Arriving at Cedar Lakes, we found that the large concrete dam that used to straddle the northeast end of the lake was now gone, allowing much more of the water to flow into the Cedar River. I had never seen the lake before, but Dad assured me that the water level was down several feet. He pointed out an entire arm of the lake that had once been submerged and now appeared as a marshy area. I wondered how it must have felt for Dad to see the differences in his old ranger territory.

Another example of the change in the woods presented itself as we passed the site of his old favorite lean-to by the dam at Cedars. The lean-to was gone, and it was now only a tent site. (He had seen this before, during his visit seven years earlier.) A single tent was set up but no one was visible, and we walked on without stopping. A new lean-to had been built at the site of the old Cedar Lakes ranger station. It seemed large, but Dad assured me that it was smaller than the old ones and that it "lacked personality." Having never seen a lean-to before, I had to take his word for it. Luckily, our destination, the Beaver Pond lean-to, was only about a quarter mile away.

The first part of the Beaver Pond lean-to that came into view was the roof. As soon as I saw it, I understood what Dad had meant when he talked about the lean-tos having personality. It was covered in a thick layer of moss and plant life. It looked as though a piece of the forest floor had been dug up and turned into a roof. As Dad walked to the front of the lean-to, I stood and admired the roof and its vegetation. Just as I finished snapping a few pictures of it, Dad shouted, "Hey, Kelly, look at this!" Walking around the side of the lean-to, I found him looking at a neat stack of new roofing materials that had been placed inside the structure. Apparently the old, mossy roof was falling apart and soon would be replaced by modern new shingles. Still, it was a shame to see the beautiful roof replaced by less interesting material.

The area surrounding Beaver Pond lean-to was also very pretty. There were many healthy white birches nearby, which was unusual, as many white birches throughout the Adirondacks and northeast have been killed by disease. A steep bank led down to the pond, and the beaver dam was visible from parts of the clearing.

As we unpacked our bags, we met a local resident. He was small, furry, and brown, and poked his nose into our lean-to to investigate the source of the noise. He was the cutest chipmunk I had ever seen. We immediately reached for our trail mix and tossed him a few peanuts. After eying them for awhile, the chipmunk (who we quickly named "Charlie") put them in his mouth and ran off, only to return, looking for more food. We spent a good deal of time feeding him unusual pieces of trail mix (probably the most unusual was a huge banana chip that was too big for his mouth) until Dad decided to collect firewood.

He walked out of the clearing and returned a few minutes later with some fairly small branches. While he broke them into pieces, he told me about all the strange things people did to start fires. I already knew most of the stories he told me, as I had read them in his books, but I let him continue. Stories about fires fueled by wood from outhouse doors are funny no matter how many times you've heard them. Unless, of course, you need to use the outhouse.

The lean-to had shelves on the inside, on which people had left unused toilet paper, twine, and other "stuff," as Dad referred to it. Among the left-behind supplies there was a plastic bag containing a soft covered notebook. "Oh, that's the lean-to journal," Dad informed me. "They put them back here for you to jot down your thoughts and observations. Why don't you look through it and add your own opinion of the woods?" I flipped through the pages, looking for interesting entries. Just a few days ago, a group with children about my age had stayed in the lean-to. I laughed as I read about their adventures (mostly concerning the chipmunk and how they had fed him all of their trail mix). Dad and I both wrote our own entries about the hike, the scenery, and (in my case) the chipmunk.

While I wrote, Dad unpacked the food for dinner. Together, we walked down to the pond to pump water with our newly purchased water purifier (a replacement for the one Dad bought several years earlier). It worked perfectly, quickly supplying us with clean, clear water for our food and canteens. After all, why wouldn't it work? Dad had tested it before we left and it had produced perfect results. Happy that the act of pumping water was accomplished so easily, we climbed back up the bank and commenced dinner preparations. We were still unaware just how troublesome that nifty device would become by the end of the week.

Dinner that night was sweet and sour chicken with apple cobbler for dessert! Both came out of a plastic bag and looked pretty much identical before water was added. Seven minutes of cooking, however, and they smelled amazing. The sweet and sour chicken was as good as it smelled. Unfortunately, the same was not true for the apple cobbler. It resembled chunks of apples floating in a grayish paste. Needless to say, I put it aside after a few bites. Dad happily ate my portion. "They should sell that stuff in stores," I said, pointing to the package of sweet and sour chicken. Dad laughed.

"They could, but I guarantee you no one would buy it. Things taste much better in the woods." I took his word for it, though I was tempted to buy another package of sweet and sour chicken when we got home, just to test his theory.

After dinner I walked to the bridge over the Beaver Pond outlet. The sun was just beginning to set, creating a beautiful scene over the pond. I took my camera with me and snapped some pictures of the landscape. (Unfortunately, I lost these pictures that night when I accidentally deleted my camera's memory.) I also took pictures of the loons swimming nearby. Dad often spoke of these beautiful, black-and-white birds, but I had never actually seen one. It seemed as though they were posing for the camera. They would swim remarkably close to the shore where I stood, sometimes disappearing underwater to fish. When they dove, they would seemingly stay under for minutes at a time, resurfacing hundreds of feet away. As they floated on the water, they produced an amazing variety of calls of varying lengths and sounds. Dad explained the difference between their calls and the purposes for each.

The quiet of the evening served to amplify the other noises around us, such as animals scurrying through the leaves near the lean-to, making them sound louder than they really were. At one point, a particularly active squirrel rustled past the back of our shelter, raising so much commotion that I thought it perhaps might be a bear. My eyes grew wide as I tried to find the source of the uproar. I peered between the back logs of the lean-to, seeing only the remains of an old blue ground cloth that had been discarded years ago.

"Oh my God, what is that?" I hollered. "It's a blue...what is it, a bear?" As soon as I said it, I realized how strange it must have sounded, but it was too late. Dad had already heard my remark—and he was going to have his fun with it.

"Forgive me, ma'am...bears don't wear blue," he replied. "But if we stick around long enough, maybe it will join us in the lean-to for some hot chocolate!" Uh huh.

As the sky grew dark, we sat in the lean-to, watching the fire. It was a beautiful night, and I was reminded of a scene from a movie. From opposite ends of the pond, loons called to one another. "Looks like we get a concert tonight," Dad said, refer-ring to the musical birds. It really did seem as though they were singing for us. Their calls probably lasted for hours. I never found out, though, because I fell asleep within minutes of crawling into my sleeping bag. I was awakened only once that night, when a mouse living in the lean-to ran across Dad's face at two o'clock. He was laughing so hard that I woke up briefly.

The next morning felt way too early. In reality, it was only six-thirty. Dad had been awake for almost two hours already and had begun to make the morning meal. Breakfast consisted of hot chocolate and oatmeal, something I'd be seeing a lot of in the next few days. I nearly choked on the oatmeal. I'm not an oat-meal lover, but this stuff was exceptionally bad. I picked at it for a while, only really eating the raisins. Luckily, the hot chocolate was wonderful and we had enough for a second cup.

Immediately after we finished eating, Dad instructed me to begin packing. As I rolled up my sleeping bag and wrestled with my stuff-sack, I noticed that Dad was packing about three times faster than me. He looked as though he could have packed blind-folded. (I remembered that he probably could have, having packed the same way hundreds of times.) Long after he finished, I was finally ready to go. We hit the trail a little after eight-thirty. I led the way, as following the trail was simple and Dad liked to hike slightly slower than me. I couldn't blame him, really. At the ripe old age (or at least it seemed so to me) of fifty-one, Dad moved a little slower than he had in his mid-twenties. He had also suffered from arthritis and had his old hip replaced with a new joint made of titanium. All in all, I found it rather impressive that he could still keep up with me.

As we came to the west end of Cedar Lakes (Third Lake, as Dad called it), we heard voices ahead. A large group came into sight, sitting on logs to the side of the trail. They introduced themselves as students from an upstate New York university. Every few minutes, they would glance down the trail ahead. They explained that they were waiting for two members of their group, one of whom had hurt his foot. Dad immediately jumped into "ranger mode," suggesting possible places to evacuate the injured person. Though he never mentioned that he had been a ranger along these same trails, the group seemed interested in his advice, and planned to evacuate the injured hiker along one of the suggested trails. As we spoke, we learned that they had planned on staying in the Third Lake lean-to, but couldn't find it. I smiled to myself as I remembered reading about Dad's attempts to locate the same lean-to in his ranger days. He gave them directions to the hidden location. Just as we started to leave, the two missing hikers returned to the group. Happy to see that they had returned safely, we said goodbye to the group and continued along the trail.

Still hiking westward, we passed some smaller ponds and marshes. It seemed that we were always walking next to some body of water. We were passing Kings Pond when we encountered a solitary male hiker. We talked for a minute or two and he told us that we were the only people he had seen in several days. Evidently the woods were relatively quiet ahead. After a short while we went on our separate ways.

My pack was starting to feel very heavy, and it was at this point when I started asking different variations of "Are we there yet?" These included "How far do you think we've walked today?" and "What time will we get there?" It was a relief to see the trail that led to the West Lake register. Unfortunately, Dad informed me that the trail was no longer usable, having been flooded out by beavers. Dad and his friend, John Remias, had tried to prevent this flooding, but the beavers had won in the end. Now hikers had to take a detour around the submerged area. "It's nothing big," Dad said cheerfully. "Just an extra half mile at most." Great. Just what I needed. The detour was hard, but the break we took at the West Lake lean-to compensated for the extra work. We still needed to hike another ten minutes to get to our final destination, the South Lake lean-to, but Dad assured me that it was an easy walk. A squirrel poked his head into the clearing and we happily shared our trail mix with him.

Dad was right: the trail to South Lake lean-to was very easy. On our way there, Dad told me about the beautiful white sand beach that lined the eastern shore of this lake. I was very excited to see this unusual sight. We crossed the bridge over the South Lake outlet, which gave us our first good look at the water. "No way," Dad muttered. I craned my neck, looking for whatever he was talking about.

"Hey, Dad, isn't there supposed to be a beach?" I asked. We both gazed at the shoreline, looking for a trace of sand. It was useless, though. Clearly the white sand beach was gone.

"It must be the beavers," Dad explained. "They built a dam which raised the water level, and they flooded the beach." Sure enough, the entire outlet of the lake was stopped up by a truly magnificent structure, about eighty feet long, with a beautiful curve arched against the current. It was an engineering marvel that must have taken months to build. But still, it had wiped out the beach that so characterized this area. I could tell Dad was pretty upset about the loss of one of his favorite locations in the region. In fact, he lamented its disappearance our entire stay at South Lake.

Even without a beach, South Lake and its lean-to were beautiful. We deposited our bags in the lean-to and immediately began our nightly chores. Dad left to search for firewood, but not before he handed me the water purifier. "Just pump the handle," he reminded me. "It shouldn't take more than five minutes to completely fill the bag." Remembering how easily we had obtained water the previous night, I took the device and skipped down to the lake. I felt a little sorry for Dad. He had to hike back down the trail, searching for firewood, while my only chore was pumping water. Smiling, I placed the end of the hose into the water and pushed down on the pump. My sympathy for Dad ended immediately. Instead of filling the bag at the end of the hose, water squirted out of the side, hitting me in the arm like a water gun. I looked at the purifier, puzzled. I must have done something wrong. Again, I pushed down on the pump and received the same result: a jet of cold water soaking my arm instead of filling the water bag.

It has been said that the definition of insanity is repeating an identical action but expecting a different result. If that is the case, I'm insane. I tried again and again to transfer water to the bag, but only succeeded in getting a very cold, very wet arm. Finally it dawned on me to pump more slowly. The water did not shoot out of the side, but it trickled into the bag at an incredibly slow rate. It was so slow that I was still pumping when Dad returned from gathering wood. "Can you tell me what I'm doing wrong?" I asked him. "I can't seem to pump the water nearly as fast as last night." Dad took the water purifier from me and headed down to the lake. He achieved the same result as I had. We even tried cleaning the filter, despite the fact that the device was new with no signs of clogging—but to no avail. I sighed. If we couldn't fix our purifier, pumping water would take a very long time (and it already had).

After what seemed like an eternity, I finally managed to pump enough water to fill the bag. I proudly presented it to Dad, who took it and began to cook dinner. While waiting to eat, I had some time to explore the area surrounding the lean-to. I decided to look for the outhouse, only to discover that there were two of them! I later had to stop Dad (and his strange sense of humor) from putting up signs labeling them "Men's" and "Women's."

The scent of dinner brought me back to the lean-to. Tonight we were having "Wild West Chili," and it smelled even better than dinner had last night. We were just sitting down to eat when we heard voices in the distance. Dad and I sat up and listened. The voices were definitely getting closer. When they approached the lean-to, we recognized them as the group from the school that we had encountered earlier that day. They had evacuated their injured friend to Cedar River Flow, where another member of their group was waiting with a car. The group asked if there were any nearby lean-tos that they could stay in. We offered them space in ours, but they politely declined. This was probably a good idea, as they had about ten people in their group, much more than the lean-to could hold. Instead, they hiked to the nearby West Canada Creek lean-to, which was less than a mile away to the south.

The chili we had for dinner was delicious and still remains my favorite meal from our trip. I finished all of mine in a hurry. While I ate, I looked out at the lake, which lapped at the shoreline just a few feet from our fireplace. There were only two loons here, but the loons on West Lake were so close that they occasionally communicated back and forth over the top of South Lake Mountain. They would also answer Dad's imitation calls!

After dinner I searched the lean-to for a journal. I was surprised to see that it was missing. "Someone probably used it to start a fire," Dad laughed. "It's amazing what people will do to avoid collecting wood." As if to prove what he had said, he pointed to part of a shelf that had clearly been broken off. "I can guarantee you that someone used that shelf for firewood, too." Wow! Somehow I couldn't imagine using part of the shelter to start a campfire. With no journal to write in, I crawled into my sleeping bag and called it an early evening.

The smell of breakfast awakened me the next morning. My stomach groaned when I remembered that breakfast would once more consist of oatmeal. Like the previous morning, I picked out the raisins and drank two glasses of hot chocolate. The sky was full of clouds, and Dad remarked several times that it looked like rain. "Don't worry," he told me. "When you're hiking underneath all of those trees, you hardly get wet." I hoped he was right. Hiking was tiring enough without being caught in a downpour. Apparently it had rained earlier that morning, too. For this reason, we were going to start our hike a little later than we had yesterday. Dad wanted to give the bushes time to dry before we started pushing our way through them. As such, we didn't hit the trail until after ten o'clock.

Dad's prediction was right: it started to rain. Unfortunately, the rain began very early in our hike, which completely defeated the purpose of waiting for the bushes to dry, as they got wet again very quickly. We left the Northville-Placid Trail just south of West Canada Creek. The new trail, which is now called the "French Louis Trail" in honor of the famous regional hermit, was noticeably smaller and less used. In a few places, it was not maintained at all. We were forced to climb over fallen trees and push through bushes that completely barricaded the path. It began to rain harder, dripping through the trees. Somehow I managed to remain dry, but Dad (who was walking in front of me) got soaked.

We passed Sampson Lake but did not head down the path to the lean-to, as we were planning to do if it were raining too hard. Fortunately, it looked as though the rain was letting up a little. We hiked on toward our original destination, Pillsbury Lake lean-to. The two lakes were very close together, so I wasn't worried that the extra distance would tire me. Once again, however, I began to feel fatigued. It felt as though every few yards we were forced to climb over or duck under a fallen tree that blocked the trail.

I was relieved to finally see Pillsbury Lake sparkling through the trees, all conifers, which thinned as we walked downhill toward the water. Situated at the bottom of the hill, the lean-to had a wonderful view of the lake, which appeared much larger than South Lake or Beaver Pond.

As soon as we reached the lean-to, we again divided up the chores. "Sorry about this," Dad chuckled, handing me the water purifier. "But someone needs to pump water." With a sigh, I took it and headed down to the lake. Pumping the water was even harder today. I watched a pair of loons swim by as I struggled with the device. After pumping for half an hour, I admitted defeat. My arms hurt and I had only managed to fill half the bag. Dad and I divided up the small amount of water between our canteens and our dinner.

We had several freeze-dried meals left in our food bag, so I requested a repeat performance of the Wild West Chili. Once again, it was fantastic. Dad also brought out a surprise: a package of foil-wrapped popcorn that supposedly popped over a campfire. We were both skeptical that it would produce anything edible. Surprisingly, it worked well, although we used our camp stove to provide the heat, and we had popcorn as an appetizer for our dinners. As we ate, the residents of the clearing (two chipmunks and a squirrel) came out of hiding. We placed a few kernels of burnt popcorn on the ground along with a small pile of trail mix. All evening they carried food away in their cheeks, and I watched them until the sun started to set. Deciding to catch up on sleep (I felt extremely tired after waking up early three consecutive mornings), I got into my sleeping bag and soon drifted off.

At first I wasn't sure what had awakened me. I knew it must have been very late, as Dad was asleep and the sky was completely dark. Then I heard it: a series of short, high-pitched squeaks, accompanied by the sound of tiny shuffling feet. Great. We had a mouse. I grabbed my flashlight and aimed it at our food bag hanging from the top of the lean-to. The small rodent was probably trying to get into it. However, when the light hit the bag, there was no mouse to be seen. I sighed and rolled over.

Wherever the mouse was, it would have to wait until morning. I was too tired to go chasing after it.

Unfortunately, as soon as I rolled over, I heard it again. *Squeak-squeak-squeak*! Then came a slightly different sound. *Squeeeeeeeeeeeeeeak*! It sounded as though the mouse was falling. Next came a soft thump as the little creature ricocheted into me. It had jumped off one of the shelves and onto my shoulder! It ran off and disappeared, leaving me laughing hysterically. I reminded myself to tell Dad about it in the morning and went back to sleep.

Even though our hike the next day was very short, we got up early in the morning. Dad wasn't sure if our dying car could make it out of the woods without breaking down, and he wanted to give us plenty of time to find help, should that happen. After our usual breakfast of oatmeal (which seemed to taste worse each day) and hot chocolate (which was as delicious as ever), we packed our bags and prepared to leave the woods. We hadn't hiked long before our trail merged with the one that had brought us into the woods. I recognized the landmarks that we had passed on our way in. Despite the bugs, the oatmeal, the water pump, the heat, and other inconveniences that had bothered me, I was truly unhappy to see that our trip was coming to an end. The trail widened into the road which led back to Sled Harbor, where our car was parked. To our astonishment, the old vehicle started on the first try, although Dad had to hammer a piece of dangling heat shield back on with a rock.

As we pulled out of the woods, Dad turned to me and asked, "So what do you think; do we come again next year?" I thought of the mosquitoes, the wet conditions, the heavy pack, and the pungent outhouses. I quickly balanced these inconveniences against the images of the beautiful lakes, the curious wildlife, the majestic mountains, and the crackling campfires at night. It was a no-brainer.

"Of course!" I answered. And I meant it.

—23—

Trail Break

As with all journeys that have a beginning and an end, this one has reached its final destination. The very act of writing about these experiences has been unforgettable, as I've been able to relive the splendor of my earlier years as a wilderness ranger in the West Canada Lakes Wilderness Area.

This endeavor has reaped benefits in so many ways that, in some regards, it has equaled my days of actually living in the woods. The very telling of each story brought back sentimental memories which had me smiling as I sat at the keyboard, recalling the people and events of the day. So many things came back, and in such surprising detail, that it felt as though the stories wrote themselves. Rather than experiencing writers' block, as it is commonly known, I often found that I couldn't write fast enough to capture my thoughts. It's easy to understand these emotions when you consider that I was working with such wonderful people in an area of incredible natural beauty. It simply doesn't get any better than that.

One of the main reasons I wanted to preserve these stories in the first place was so that my daughters could read about them after I'm gone. (As an older parent, I worried about that for quite a while.) Little could I have known that I would have the joy of taking my older daughter on a personally-guided tour of my old stomping grounds, as I did in the summer of 2007. I was able to show her how a beaver builds its lodge, how to keep a fire going in the rain, and how to identify the different songs of the loons on the lake. This is the stuff that forges memories for a lifetime, and I will treasure it forever.

The desire to act as a guide for Kelly during our trip through the West Canada Lakes may have also been a catalyst for me to take action on my physical disability. I had been severely limited by a badly arthritic hip for four years and would have been unable to even attempt this trek without the miracle of modern surgery. So, in the spring of 2005, I underwent hip replacement surgery and had a completely artificial hip installed. I was restored to 100% of my pre-arthritic condition, and thus able to make this trip. I carried a sixty-pound pack for four days through wet and hilly terrain without a trace of my former discomfort. Without the incentive of this sentimental return to my territory, I might have been tempted to delay that surgery until later in life. Instead, I have the ability to hike and climb with unencumbered mobility, for which I am eternally grateful.

Another advantage to writing these books has been that it has brought me back in touch with a whole part of my life, including the many friends and acquaintances I made while living in the North Country. This aspect is certainly bittersweet, because so many of my older friends (as well as some of the younger ones) have now passed away. Some of these people, including John Remias and Leighton Slack, were such good friends and companions that their absence has left a hole that will be impossible to fill. Thankfully, I do have a great many wonderful friends who still live and work in that area, and these books have allowed me to reconnect with many of them.

One unexpected benefit of recording these episodes has been

the warm and lasting relationship that I've developed with many other Adirondack authors. The Adirondack Park is so large and diverse, and has such a fantastic history, that it has spawned literally hundreds of regional writers. This is a wonderful and important thing, because these talented individuals have preserved the story of our greatest natural resource. To a person, each of these writers is not only a gifted literary artist, but also well versed in his or her own niche of Adirondack lore. To read their stories, whether they are historical, folklore, or just plain fiction, gives me great pleasure and has filled many of my spare hours with joy. Even more so, I have enjoyed our friendships, which would have been impossible if not for my own entrance into this noble pastime of Adirondack writing.

Finally, the greatest part of these past few years has been my interactions with the readers of these books. This relationship has been rewarding on so many levels that it is difficult to summarize concisely. On a technical level, many readers have contacted me to provide comments and suggestions about specific places mentioned in these stories. To all of them I extend a heartfelt "thank you." I also appreciate those readers who have told me about the joy that they have found while sharing these stories with their children. I am thrilled when people express pleasure they've experienced from reading these chronicles themselves, but to share them with "the little ones" serves to enhance both their love of reading as well as their appreciation of our Adirondack Park. These are highly worthy endeavors, and I am truly honored that I've been permitted to play a role in both.

Other readers have written me to ask a number of questions, two of which appear on a regular basis. The first of these is, did these stories really happen to you, and second, will there be a fourth book? I can answer both of these together, because they are actually two parts of the same question. Yes, these episodes happened, for the most part, as I described, although I have occasionally used a small degree of "literary license" to enhance an event or personality. But I am a strong believer that "truth is stranger than fiction," which is evident throughout the chapters of my life from this era. As such, there was simply no need to invent any stories; they really happened, and all I had to do was to record what I saw.

Another reason I tried to keep these volumes as real (or "anecdotal") as possible was that I wanted to record the stories of my life for my daughters to read in the decades after I am gone. Developing fictional stories simply would not have been appropriate for this purpose, and so I never seriously considered moving in that direction.

The answer to the second question (about a potential fourth book), is no. I am pleased to say that I have been able to fill these three volumes with stories of real people and places that were very near and dear to me, and for that I am grateful. However, I have reached the end of my recollections of my life in the woods, and I have fully described every colorful event from that three year period. In order to go on from here, I would have to write fiction, and I simply do not want to go there.

However, rather than call this the "end of the trail," I'd rather think of it as a lengthy rest stop. I say this because of the potential to someday return to the backcountry and meet more new friends with even more stories. This circle is endless, because these woods we call the Adirondacks will be there forever, even if we are not. As long as people are able to return to these woods and sit around the fire at night, stories will be exchanged. These books have merely given me the opportunity and medium to pass my experiences along to a larger audience.

With this in mind, I'll conclude by saying that I hope we get to meet one another and trade stories in just such a place, nestled around a glowing fire in front of an Adirondack lean-to deep in the north woods. Our woods; our Adirondacks. Until then, may the sun always shine on your path, may the trout always rise to your line, and may the flames of your fire never die.

About the Authors

Larry Weill has led a career that is as diverse and interesting as the subjects in his books. An avid outdoorsman, he has hiked and climbed extensively throughout the Adirondacks and the Northeast since his days as a wilderness park ranger. He has also worked as a financial planner, a technical writer, a trainer, and a career Naval officer.

A self-avowed "people watcher," Larry has an interesting knack for observing and describing people and their many amusing habits and traits. He is the author of *Excuse Me, Sir...Your Socks are on Fire* and *Pardon Me, Sir... There's a Moose in Your Tent* (North Country Books, Inc.).

Larry lives in Rochester, New York, with his wife and two daughters. They vacation and hike in the Adirondacks annually.

Kelly Weill is a high school student in Upstate New York. She has been writing for several years, and has published several articles online. She is a member of her school soccer and track teams, along with numerous other clubs and activities. She looks forward to a career in writing and journalism.